Classrooms of possibility

Supporting at-risk EAL students

Edited by

Jennifer Hammond
and Jennifer Miller

PETAA
PRIMARY ENGLISH TEACHING
ASSOCIATION AUSTRALIA

First published 2015
Primary English Teaching Association Australia (PETAA)
Laura St, Newtown, NSW 2042, Australia
PO Box 3106, Marrickville Metro, NSW 2204
Tel: (02) 8020 3900
Fax: (02) 8020 3933
Email: info@petaa.edu.au
Website: www.petaa.edu.au
ISBN 978-1-925132-19-9

National Library of Australia Cataloguing-in-Publication entry (pbk)
Creator: Hammond, Jennifer, author, editor.

Title: Classrooms of possibility : supporting at-risk EALstudents / Jennifer Hammond, Jenny Miller, authors and editors; contributors, Jacquie Coleman, Maya Cranitch, Miranda McCallum, Jonnell Uptin, Karen Dooley.
ISBN: 9781925132199 (paperback)

Notes: Includes bibliographical references.
Subjects: Second language acquisition. English language--Study and teaching--Foreign speakers. English language--Acquisition. Literacy--Australia.

Other Creators/Contributors: Miller, Jenny, author, editor.
Coleman, Jacquie. Cranitch, Maya.
McCallum, Miranda. Uptin, Jonnell.
Primary English Teaching Association (Australia)
Dewey Number: 428.24

Cover and internal design by Toni Darben, Darben Design
Edited and project managed by Rema Gnanadickam, Zodiac Publishing Services
Printed in Australia by Ligare Pty Ltd.

Contents

Acknowledgements

The author and publisher gratefully acknowledge the use of the following copyright material in this publication:

UNHCR for images on pages 14, 15, 20 and 28; UNCEF for images on pages 17 & 18, Maya Cranitch for images on pages 20, 23 and 28; Cromer Public School, NSW for image on page 28; and Jennifer Miller for images on page 116.

While every effort has been made to trace and acknowledge copyright and ownership of all included works, should any infringement have occurred, the publisher offers their apologies and invite copyright owners to contact them.

The contributors

Maya Cranitch is currently coordinator of the Australian Catholic University Refugee Project on the Thai–Burma Border. With long standing experience working in the refugee sector both in Australia and overseas, Maya has for fifteen years been a Board member of the Asylum Seekers' Centre in Sydney. She has conducted workshops for the Refugee Council of Australia, mentored several Sudanese university students and presented at a UNHCR sponsored Round Table in Geneva. She has worked closely with the NSW Department of Education and Communities to develop the teacher education resource: *Teaching Refugees in My Classroom*. Maya also lectures in the area of teaching literacy and English as an additional language in the Faculty of Education and Social Work at the University of Sydney.

Jacqueline Coleman is a former mainstream primary teacher who taught in both rural and non-metropolitan areas in Australia. Her interest in EAL-related issues began when she had a lone newly-arrived EAL learner in her composite Year 3 /4 class. As professional learning to support mainstream teachers with at-risk EAL students was not available, she undertook further study to find some practical solutions to working effectively with her EAL student. Having also worked as an EAL teacher of newly-arrived adult refugees and migrants in Australia and in teacher education programmes in Latin America and Africa, she now co-ordinates and teaches undergraduate and post-graduate EAL courses at the Australian Catholic University in Sydney. She researches and publishes on ways to support teachers at all levels of education, including those in rural and non-metropolitan areas, to meet the challenges of successfully teaching EAL students.

Karen Dooley is an Associate Professor in the School of Curriculum, Faculty of Education, Queensland University of Technology. Karen began her career in Australia teaching in linguistically and culturally diverse schools in high-poverty areas and also taught English as a foreign language in a Shanghai middle school. She currently teaches English Curriculum studies in the primary pre-service teacher education program. Her special interest is in literacy education in conditions of linguistic and cultural diversity. She supervises research projects concerned with language and literacy education for EAL and EFL students. Karen's Australian Research Council-funded studies have looked at pedagogy for adolescents of refugee background, and print and digital literacies in a high-poverty, high-diversity primary school.

Miranda McCallum is a specialist (EAL) classroom teacher and curriculum leader. She spent two years working on the ARC Linkage project with Jenny Miller and Joel Windle, and has written targeted curriculum material combining science content with language goals. She has presented to pre-service students and teachers, and currently works as an Education Consultant assisting schools to implement Peer Support and other leadership programs.

Jonnell Uptin lectures in Literacy and Diversity at University of Sydney and also coordinates programs for international students at University of Wollongong. Jonnell spent her career as a teacher in ESL, music and as a classroom teacher in Australia, Singapore and Thailand. While teaching in Thailand she spent 8 years volunteering in an orphanage for children living with HIV and worked with refugees from Burma. Jonnell visits Northern Thailand regularly, offering educational expertise to programs that assist both Thai and stateless mothers enabling them to keep and care for their children.

1

At-risk EAL students in mainstream classrooms

Jennifer Hammond & Jennifer Miller

The purpose of this book

This book draws together recent work from a number of researchers and educators who have focused on the successes, needs, and challenges of 'at-risk' English as an Additional Language (EAL) students in Australian schools. In broad terms, the category of 'at-risk' students includes those from refugee backgrounds, and EAL students who have had minimal or disrupted schooling prior to arriving in Australia.

The book has three main aims. These are:

- To address the needs of at-risk EAL students once they are integrated into mainstream classes. Although many EAL students attend intensive language programs or specialist English centres when they have newly arrived in Australia, our concern in this book is with what happens in mainstream classrooms when at-risk EAL students must engage in the full school curriculum, and when specialist support may be limited or withdrawn.
- To focus on teaching and learning practices within mainstream classes that are likely to support at-risk EAL students to engage fully and equitably in the school curriculum. By focusing on teaching and learning practices, we aim to provide both theoretical and practical insights, ideas and strategies for primary and middle year teachers working with at-risk EAL students in English and other subject areas.
- To address the specific needs of at-risk EAL students by proposing ways in which teachers can better support such students to develop academic language and literacy. In doing so, we aim to complement the Australian Curriculum (ACARA, 2012) and its accompanying EAL Resource document (ACARA, 2011). Chapters in the book thus complement the Curriculum as a whole, and they complement, in particular, the English Curriculum, with its strands of Language and Literacy.

The intended readers of this book are mainstream teachers and specialist EAL teachers of both primary and middle years – that is, teachers who are working with at-risk EAL students in their classrooms. However, we hope that the various chapters will also be of value for administrators, teacher educators and academics in the fields of EAL, TESOL and literacy education. While intended primarily for an Australian audience, we believe the theoretical and practical insights provided by the various chapters in the book are likely to be relevant for those working with at-risk EAL students in other English-speaking countries.

Who are at-risk EAL students?

We use the term 'at risk' to refer to EAL students from refugee backgrounds, and to those who have experienced minimal or disrupted schooling prior to arriving in Australia. Such students are likely to be 'at risk' of educational failure for two reasons:

1 Their experiences of disruption and trauma prior to arrival in Australia may make their transition to life in Australia, including schooling, particularly challenging.
2 Disrupted or limited access to formal schooling prior to arrival in Australia may mean students have significant gaps in educational knowledge and conceptual development. They are also likely to have limited literacy abilities in their mother tongue or additional languages. On commencing school in Australia, students face the challenge, not only of learning English language and literacy, but also of closing substantial gaps between their educational knowledge and that of their Australian peers.

Every year, Australia accepts an ongoing quota of around 13 000 new arrivals of people on special humanitarian visas (from both off-shore and on-shore streams). In 2012–13, the main source countries were Iraq, Afghanistan, Burma, Bhutan, and the Democratic Republic of Congo (Department of Immigration and Border Protection, Canberra, 2013). Other source countries included Iran, Somalia, Sudan, Eritrea and Ethiopia, although this list may change from year to year depending on where the greatest humanitarian crisis is at any one time. While it is difficult to obtain accurate data on the precise numbers of students of refugee background in Australian schools, and to gauge the numbers of refugee-background students as a proportion of the more general body of EAL students, we do know that New South Wales and Victoria accept roughly a third each of Australia's new immigrant arrivals, including refugees, with the remaining third going to other states and territories.

The political upheaval and conflict evident in the major source countries of people arriving on humanitarian visas makes it certain that the majority of refugee students will arrive with interrupted schooling. In addition, particularly in recent years, some students have fled their homes, seen family members killed, or lived for lengthy periods in dangerous camps and transition sites (including detention). Many have experienced severe trauma before arriving in Australia. On arrival, they may continue to live in precarious circumstances, with little family support or inadequate resources. As one state government EAL Report notes:

> Over the past 10 years, the national origin of refugee and humanitarian entrants has changed substantially, resulting in many of the students who are now enrolled having had severely interrupted schooling or little or no experience of school. The lack of literacy in a first or a second language, little or no knowledge or understanding of how school works, and the trauma associated with the refugee experience, means that refugee students are likely to face substantial obstacles to settling, including learning in our schools (DEECD, 2008).

At-risk EAL students, however, are not a homogenous group. They are diverse in ways that other groups of students are diverse. Some students may have had extensive formal schooling prior to being impacted by war. These students may be highly literate in their mother tongues and have a strong basis for ongoing education in Australia. Others may have had access to some schooling in different countries prior to arriving in Australia. Many will be familiar with at least conversational levels of several languages. The use of terms such as 'refugee' and 'at risk' can therefore be problematic. Such labels tend to position students as victims and to highlight the problems associated with students' journeys to Australia and their subsequent settlement in Australia. As is evident in the further chapters of this book, students themselves resist such positioning. Their concern is primarily with the future, and most students look forward with energy and enthusiasm to positive participation in school and in the broader Australian society. However, while some of the specific issues and challenges students face will overlap with those faced by other EAL students, at-risk students differ in the trauma often associated with their journey to Australia, and in the ongoing settlement struggle faced by their families or carers. The result is that issues and challenges confronted by students may be magnified.

In this book, we use the term 'at risk' to acknowledge the specific challenges students face as they engage in education in their first years in Australia. These challenges include, initially, the cultural and social adjustments necessary for participation at school and within the broader Australian society. They include, most obviously, the learning of English language and literacy, but also the development of educational concepts that may already be very familiar to their peers.

As indicated earlier in this introduction, our particular concern in the book is with students of a refugee background, and with other EAL students who may have experienced minimal or disrupted schooling prior to coming to Australia. For this reason, we use the term EAL rather than English as an Additional Language/Dialect (EAL/D) in the book. However, we are aware that other groups of students may be considered 'at risk' of educational failure at school. EAL students from lower socio-economic backgrounds, including those born in Australia as well as those born overseas, who experience difficulties with English literacy, may be considered 'at risk'. Although such students are not the central focus of this book, the theoretical principles and practical teaching/learning strategies addressed in the various chapters of the book, we would argue, are also relevant for teachers working with such students in their classrooms.

Educational challenges for students, their teachers and schools

Educational challenges faced by at-risk EAL students who have: limited or no previous education; and little or no literacy experience in their first language (or in any language) are extensive. Specific challenges include: unfamiliarity with school routines and classroom practices; conceptual difficulties and limited prior knowledge to relate to new topics; minimal print literacy; and embarrassment about comparisons with mainstream peers.

There is consistent evidence that the strongest predictor of educational success for students learning in a second (or additional) language is the level of formal education in their first language (Thomas & Collier, 1997). A key element of formal education is literacy development. For students who are not literate in their first language, learning school English, which assumes so much about previous literate practice, will be many times harder than for those who can read and write their first language. For many such students, their classroom may be their first encounter with print materials. As a result, they may have a range of high-level needs related to second language and literacy, conceptual and content knowledge, as well as behavioural, welfare and social needs. Despite the obstacles they face, with high levels of targeted educational support, many at-risk EAL students can, and do, make remarkable progress and achieve academic success. The students' own resilience and determination contribute to this success.

The presence of at-risk EAL students in mainstream classes, however, clearly presents additional challenges for schools and for teachers. As indicated, many students bring very different levels of educational knowledge to the classroom, and often have very different language and educational needs from those of mainstream English-speaking students. The particular challenge for schools and for teachers is to address the needs of these students, while at the same time continuing to meet the needs of other groups of students within their classes. Our aim in this book is to provide support for schools and teachers in addressing this challenge.

It is often assumed that numbers of at-risk EAL students in schools are relatively small, and that their education, at least in their first years of schooling in Australia, is primarily the responsibility of specialist EAL teachers. Recent changes in education, migration and settlement policies challenge that assumption.

Changes in education policy at both Commonwealth and state levels have significant consequences for schools and teachers. An emphasis on increased school autonomy and financial responsibility, along with changes in funding and responsibility for EAL programs, has meant that schools across Australian states now have increasing responsibility, not only for overall functioning of schools, but also for the organisation and funding of EAL support. One consequence of these changes is that mainstream class and subject teachers are required to assume a greater responsibility than in previous years for the education of all students in their classes, including at-risk EAL students. This responsibility includes support for *all* students' language and literacy learning development across the curriculum in mainstream classes.

Changes in migration and settlement policies have also impacted on schools. For many years, refugee background and other at-risk EAL students have tended to be clustered in disadvantaged schools in low socio-economic areas in major cities. However, in recent years, increasing numbers of students and their families have settled in regional areas of Australia. The consequence is that some schools and teachers with little prior experience of working with EAL students are faced with the need to develop programs and teaching strategies that meet the needs of these students. While the inclusion of at-risk EAL students does not impact on every school or on every teacher, the overall consequence of policy changes is that the majority of teachers, at some points in their careers, will work with at-risk students.

Why the focus on pedagogy?

A quick review of the related literature shows that there has (rightly) been considerable prior emphasis on the wellbeing and welfare of at-risk students (Vickers, 2007; Matthews, 2008). To date, however, there has been less emphasis on the kinds of teaching and learning practices that will best support students in their attempts to engage with Australian schooling (Hammond, 2014a; Windle & Miller, 2012). A consistent request from many mainstream teachers is for information and help regarding the kinds of teaching practices that will better support their at-risk EAL students.

Our overall focus in this book is on the nature of classrooms and pedagogical practices that are most likely to provide at-risk EAL students both with access to key educational concepts, and with the kind of support that makes it possible for them to engage with those concepts and make progress at school. We recognise that without the prior provision of a supportive and positive learning environment where students feel safe and valued, little constructive learning is possible. Chapters of this book build on this recognition, but focus on students' educational progress and on teaching and learning practices that make educational progress possible.

Equity in education, language and learning

An important principle that guided the development of the Australian Curriculum was as stated here:

> One important lesson learned from past efforts to overcome inequality is that an alternative curriculum for students regarded as disadvantaged does not treat them equitably. It is better to set the same high expectations for all students and to provide differentiated levels of support to ensure that all students have a fair chance to achieve those expectations. (ACARA, 2009, p. 8)

This statement reflects the views expressed by the authors in this book – that all students, including at-risk EAL students, should have access to a full curriculum. A modified or less challenging curriculum for any student restricts that student's access to an equitable education. There is consistent evidence to suggest that like other students, EAL students benefit from high-challenge programs. The work of Newmann and his associates (Newmann, Marks & Gamoran, 1996) provides evidence that programs characterised by high intellectual challenge have a positive impact on the educational achievement of ***all*** students, including those from diverse social, linguistic and cultural backgrounds, and that, as a result of engagement with such programs, the equity gap between students is reduced. Such evidence is consistent with the extensive literature on teacher expectations that indicates all students, including those who are linguistically and culturally diverse, achieve higher educational outcomes when teachers' expectations are high (Carrasquillo & London, 1993; Darling-Hammond & Schon, 1996).

While most Australian teachers and educators are likely to support the principle that equitable education requires access to a full curriculum, they are also likely to be very aware of the practical challenges associated with its implementation. A consistent complaint of many teachers, including those from upper primary and the middle years of high school, is that they are forced to balance the pressure to 'get through the curriculum content', with attempting to develop programs that genuinely aim for engagement with key educational concepts and curriculum knowledge. This pressure is particularly problematic for those trying to implement pedagogical practices that allow time for at-risk EAL students to engage at a deep level with curriculum knowledge. While we recognise the nature of this challenge, we believe the answer lies in increasing the levels of differentiated support (which for some students, may include initial modification of tasks), rather than in reducing the expectations of what students can achieve. Indeed there is evidence that students themselves support this view. As one student of refugee background commented when discussing her progress in high school:

. . . the important thing is, are you going forward or are you going back?

In various ways, the chapters of this book address ways in which students can be supported to 'go forward' within the context of mainstream classes. In Australia, as elsewhere, Vygotskian theories (see Vygotsky, 1978) regarding the social nature of learning have impacted on our understanding of high-support learning environments. A key element here has been the role of scaffolding in constructing such environments (Gibbons, 2002; 2009a; Hammond & Gibbons, 2005). The concept of scaffolding is taken up by a number of authors in this book to articulate how teachers can build-in differential levels of support for their EAL students, including their at-risk EAL students, to enable students to engage with challenging curriculum concepts.

Chapters in this book also make the point that high-support learning environments require teachers to draw on similar theoretical understandings of language and literacy and of learning as they would for other students. Such environments require teachers to draw from a broad repertoire of teaching strategies and tasks as they would for other students. As a number of authors point out, where responses to the needs of at-risk students differ is in the selection and sequencing of tasks and strategies in small learning steps to ensure students have access to targeted support that pushes them to work just beyond their comfort levels. Pedagogical practices that support at-risk students will require a more explicit and targeted language focus, more emphasis on building cultural and background knowledge, and more carefully paced sequences of learning tasks, but at the same time are not different in kind from practices that support many other students.

Support for academic language and literacy development

The most obvious area of need for at-risk EAL students is support for English language and literacy development, and virtually all teachers recognise this priority. Teachers consistently identify support for English language and literacy development as the most pressing need for EAL students, and especially for at-risk EAL students (Watkins et al., 2013). However, many mainstream teachers lack the necessary confidence and knowledge to provide adequate levels of such support (Hammond, 2008; Macken-Horarik, Love & Unsworth, 2011; Jones & Chen, 2012). While some specialist EAL teachers have extensive knowledge of language and language development, the majority of classroom and subject teachers have had limited access to the kind of professional support that would enable them to develop such knowledge. Most teachers report attempting to address aspects of language and literacy within programs, however, such teaching is generally limited to the more accessible levels of vocabulary or spelling and punctuation. What is missing is more consistent, systematic and in-depth teaching across the curriculum of different levels of language: at the levels of text organisation; cohesion; paragraph organisation; sentence grammar; as well as at levels of vocabulary; punctuation and spelling (Macken-Horarik, Love & Unsworth, 2011; Jones & Chen, 2012).

The knowledge required to provide this level of support in academic language and literacy development is extensive. As Cummins (2000; 2008), Gibbons (2009), and others have pointed out, English academic language and literacy development is considerably more challenging than learning conversational skills in a language. Most EAL students are able to learn basic communication skills in English relatively quickly. Indeed many at-risk EAL students already have communicative proficiency in the several languages they have encountered in refugee camps and other locations during their journey between their own country and Australia. After a year or so of living in Australia and attending school, most appear reasonably fluent in conversational English – they are able to understand classroom directions, buy food in shops, negotiate public transport, engage in conversations and arguments with their peers and engage in sports activities. They have reasonable control of what Cummins (2008) refers to as Basic Interpersonal Communication Skills (BICS).

The development of BICS represents an important achievement for any student, but is it not enough. As students engage at deeper levels with curriculum knowledge across the years of primary school and into secondary, they need to develop increasing control of academic language and literacy. In the terms of Cummins (2008), they need to develop control of Cognitive Academic Language Proficiency (CALP). This involves what Gibbons (2009a) refers to as 'literate talk', as well as control of academic literacy in discipline-specific areas. That is, students need to develop control of specific registers as well as key genres within subject areas; they need to engage with subject-specific ways of talking about educational concepts; they need to develop understandings of written genres, with their distinctive rhetorical structures and grammatical patterns, and they need to engage with a range of multimodal texts. As students work their way through school they are required to read texts where information and arguments are organised in ways that differ from spoken language (whether that be everyday or literate talk), and they need insights into the increasingly abstract and metaphorical language of academic written texts, and into ways in which language and literacy differ across different curriculum areas (Gibbons, 2002; 2009; Macken-Horarik, Love & Unsworth, 2011; Jones & Chen, 2012). Most students require support to develop understandings of across-the-curriculum academic language and literacy. For at-risk EAL students who have had little prior access to schooling, including literacy development in their mother tongue, the task is that much greater (Miller, Mitchell & Brown, 2005; Windle & Miller, 2012).

The demands of language and literacy development across the curriculum have been acknowledged in the Australian Curriculum. While these demands are addressed most explicitly in the subject English through the Language and Literacy strands (ACARA, 2011), the importance of supporting language and literacy more broadly is also recognised in curriculum documents for other subjects. However, while curriculum documents from subjects other than English acknowledge the importance of language across the curriculum, they provide little explicit support for teachers in how to do this (Hammond, 2012). The chapters in this book thus complement the Australian Curriculum by contributing to understandings of ways in which the teaching of academic language and literacy can be integrated with the teaching of key concepts across the curriculum. They also provide insights into how the targeted efforts of schools and teachers can assist at-risk students to achieve their educational potential.

Contributors to this book

Following this introductory chapter, Chapters 2 and 3 focus on the nature, experiences and voices of at-risk EAL students, especially those from refugee backgrounds. In Chapter 2, Maya Cranitch draws on her many years of experience in teaching and research with students from a refugee background, both internationally and in Australia, to provide insights into their lives and educational experiences prior to arrival in Australia. Her chapter addresses the complexity and limitations of education in a resource-poor context where there are few trained teachers, and no clearly articulated curriculum. It also provides insights into the nature and extent of cultural, social, educational and linguistic adjustment required of students when they begin school in Australia. In Chapter 3, Jonnell Uptin addresses the experiences of students at school in Australia. She highlights the diversity of backgrounds of at-risk EAL students, and the nature of the students' positive energy and agency in negotiating their own places in Australian schools. The chapter also highlights the role of schools in promoting inclusion for at-risk EAL students, and ways in which teachers can learn from, and respond to, their students. Both chapters respond in different ways to common requests from teachers for more information about the background and experiences of their at-risk EAL students. By contributing to a better understanding of students, and of what students bring with them to school, the chapters aim to help teachers work effectively in their classes with at-risk EAL students.

The remaining chapters of the book, Chapters 4, 5, 6 and 7, all address pedagogical practices that are likely to support at-risk EAL students in various ways. In Chapter 4, Jacqueline Coleman draws on her research in non-metropolitan primary schools into the nature of mainstream teachers' responses to their at-risk EAL students. Since teachers who participated in the research had had little prior experience of EAL education, it was not surprising that their responses to at-risk EAL students primarily involved 'pastoral' care. The chapter highlights the challenges faced by teachers who are expected 'to cope' with the arrival of students of refugee background in their classes, and it address some of the pedagogical implications for other teachers working with at-risk EAL students in primary schools. In Chapter 5, Jennifer Hammond also draws on research into current teaching-learning practices. Her research focused on the experiences of middle year at-risk EAL students both before and after their transition from an Intensive English Centre to high school. The research highlighted important strengths in current practices, but also identified a number of ways in which they could be further strengthened to support at-risk EAL students more effectively. The chapter has implications for schools interested in the analysis and refinement of existing pedagogical practices.

While Chapters 4 and 5 are primarily based on research into the nature of current teaching and learning practices, Chapters 6, 7 and 8 focus on implications and possible ways forward for those working with at-risk EAL students. In Chapter 5, Jennifer Miller and Miranda McCallum build on outcomes from a large research project to address pedagogical implications of working with low-level literacy students in the middle years of schooling. They outline a 'literacy model' that is designed to help teachers address the specific needs of students with low levels of literacy (in their mother tongues as well as in English). The chapter provides suggestions for mainstream teachers in regard to the planning and sequencing of activities with the necessary small steps to support students' learning in the foundational elements of literacy. These small steps are integral to students' acquisition of language and their participation in critical and evaluative tasks. In Chapter 7, Karen Dooley focuses on the nature of pedagogy that engages and supports at-risk primary students. Through her analysis of an after-school Media Club, her chapter highlights the power of multimodality to engage at-risk EAL students in learning, and the overall importance of multimodal literacy for primary school students. Chapters 6 and 7 build on outcomes from specific research projects to address implications for working with at-risk EAL students. Chapter 8 addresses pedagogical practices directly. In this chapter, Jennifer Miller provides a set of principles and practical suggestions for supporting students to access the curriculum, while also ensuring they are working in a context where expectations and challenges remain high.

Finally, in Chapter 9 Jennifer Hammond provides a brief summary of major themes and lessons learned from the book as a whole. The focus of this chapter is on implications and ways forward in regard to pedagogies that support and challenge at-risk EAL students in the primary and middle years of schooling.

2

Refugees bring more than they can carry

Maya Cranitch

Teachers have often indicated that they have no real idea of what their students have experienced prior to their arrival in an Australian school. In this chapter, I draw on my years of working with children and families of refugee backgrounds and on my experiences as coordinator of the Australian Catholic University Diploma of Liberal Studies program on the Thailand/Myanmar border to provide readers with more information about the types of experiences that students may have had.

My focus is specifically on refugee students. Refugees fleeing from persecution can carry little that is material: instead they bring a determination to survive; a spirit of resilience and hope in the future. The small children playing with stones in the dust, the people rebuilding homes after each wet season washes away houses and bridges in a refugee camp, or the single mothers coping with the awesome demands of managing a family in a new culture testify to hope in the future.

Mainstream teachers tend to be more familiar with migrant EAL learners with continuous and settled education backgrounds. However, teachers may not realise what disrupted or non-formal education means for the development of age-appropriate skills and knowledge, which is often the refugee students' experience. This chapter explores and contextualises some of the experiences of learners from refugee backgrounds prior to their arrival in Australian schools. To this end, I draw on two case studies of Syrian refugees in Jordan and refugees in Thailand from Myanmar (or 'Burma' as the Australian Government and most Burmese use to refer to their country), to provide insights into education in both emergency and protracted refugee situations. These case studies not only provide important information, but also suggest the types of questions teachers might ask about individual learners' backgrounds. I conclude the chapter by addressing some key implications for teachers to consider in the provision of high-challenge high-support teaching and learning for students from refugee backgrounds.

Who are refugees?

The refugee experience is always complex, pitching ordinary people into extraordinary situations involving violence or threats of violence, fear and intimidation. Refugees are frequently members of a minority, whether because of race, ethnicity, religion or sexual orientation. Perhaps they were politically active, opposing an authoritarian regime, or they may just as well have been relatives of activists or just bystanders swept up in the violence of a war or conflict.

Jeffrey Stern (*The Atlantic*, May 21, 2013) explains the situation of Afghan Hazaras 'the most persecuted ethnic group on the planet' like this:

> You are Muslim, but you are Shia. What this means is that in Afghanistan, you believed in the right God, but the wrong way. In Iran you believed the right way, but looked wrong. In Iraq, and now in Syria, you were wrong in both ways.

The world population of refugees and displaced people was estimated to be over 51 million at the end of 2013 (UNHCR, June 2014). This is not a homogeneous population but includes rich and poor, well-educated professionals and illiterate rural villagers as well as families of all shapes and sizes. A Syrian medical doctor may have little in common with an illiterate labourer fleeing the same bombs, or a Christian Pakistani businessman facing religious persecution from the Taliban, or a farmer from Karen state in Myanmar whose village has been burned, or a Nuer family in Kakuma Camp in Kenya waiting to see if the latest peace treaty holds in Southern Sudan. Individual experiences, life stories and future expectations should be acknowledged and never overlooked.

The following recount illustrates how quickly one child's life is disrupted forever:

Nidal's story

Six-year old Nidal and his sister fled the conflict in Syria because of ongoing shelling and shooting. He was shot at while playing in the street with friends, was chased, and witnessed armed men taking his father away. His father was then killed in the street.

"My name is Nidal. I am six years old. I left Syria eight days ago. What do I remember? Shelling. And explosions. Houses fell, all because of an explosion. Another house was hit and was destroyed completely. There were people inside. [My grandma's] house is filled with bullet holes, even the steel doors were broken. Men were running and shooting. A man came to our house, opened the door violently and sat next to our window with his rifle. And they all started shooting. I was scared. I was scared when I saw the fire. I thought maybe the house would burn while we were inside. I thought I was going to die. My message to the world? The war should stop in Syria so we can go back to our country."

The refugee journey

While there are common themes in refugees' flights towards saftey, their journey is rarely predictable and almost never an orderly movement from a place of fear to a place of safety. It may involve:

- sudden departures with no time for preparation, leaving family members behind or losing them on the way
- hazardous travel in unsafe vehicles through dangerous territory without any idea of the journey's end
- names and personal information, often the very cause of persecution, may need to be abandoned in favour of false documents
- re-assigned family relationships and invented pasts created in order to disguise identity and minimise discovery.

In fact, many people from developing countries do not have official identity papers: they may not know their date of birth or they may have little understanding of the role and significance of formal documents. For example, when the group of children and adolescents known as the 'lost boys' of South Sudan arrived in Kenyan refugee camps, their ages were estimated according to wrist size, and all were given the same birth date: January first.

Throughout the refugee journey, children are usually left in the dark to draw their own conclusions from events that overtake them like a sudden departure in the night or the disappearance of a parent. Added to the terror of immediate events is the realisation that the adult world is out of control, unsafe and insecure. The overwhelming impression of stories about the refugee journey is one of such chaos and confusion that the unimaginable becomes possible: children can be separated from parents and so lose their identity. Naomi Steer, writing from Kenya for UNHCR (United Nations High Commissioner for Refugees) Australia, states that there are about 13 000 unaccompanied minors in the Kakuma camp, one of the largest and oldest refugee camps, which was home to many refugees who eventually resettled in Australia (Steer, 2014). She recounts the following:

> One boy holds a neatly typed card with the following information:
>
> *Name: Suleiman*
> *Nationality: Darfurian*
> *Age: Not Sure*

> *I have been kidnapped in Darfur as a two-year-old boy and taken to the Central African Republic where I was trained as a soldier. Life was miserable and I often ate only leaves. I was rescued by UNMID (the United Nationals Mission in Darfur) and taken to Juba in South Sudan. I was born in Jebel Mara. If you can help with my identity, contact Darfurian Chief)*

The refugee journey almost always involves lengthy periods of transit waiting in refugee camps or in unwelcoming urban areas. Refugee camps, despite popular belief, are not places of safety. Shifting populations from different ethnic and religious groups are crowded together, absolutely dependent on aid agencies for food and shelter and kept in a state of suspended animation (see Figures 2.1 and 2.2). Processing by UNHCR to determine refugee status sometimes takes years and the opportunities for either repatriation or resettlement are often limited.

The situation for refugees in countries of first asylum depends largely on the attitude of the host country. Work rights, access to aid agencies, health and education services vary dramatically. Refugees in urban areas such as the Afghan Hazaras in Pakistan, the

Figure 2.1: Somali refugees in Dollo Ado Camp, Ethiopia

Figure 2.2: Syrian refugees amongst UNHCR tents at the Zaatari refugee camp, Jordanian city of Mafraq, near Syrian border

Pakistanis in Bangkok or the Rohingya in Malaysia face challenges that are different, but no less difficult, than those faced by inmates of camps. Processing of urban refugees is even more haphazard than in the camps, especially in those countries not signatories to the UN Convention. According to Fr John Murray (Director of the National Catholic Commission on Migration, Thailand), in personal communication in 2014, UNHCR now estimates that refugees and asylum seekers living illegally in Bangkok may be waiting for up to ten years before resettlement. Without social or legal protection, urban refugees face constant threats from hostile locals and police, fear of discovery and consequent deportation as well as the struggle to maintain livelihoods. Often these fears prevent parents from sending children to school even when, in theory, access is possible.

Access to education for refugee children

There are different challenges in providing access to education in refugee camps and urban settings. These challenges relate to the attitudes of the host government, the role of aid agencies, the physical infrastructure as well as the skills and resources available in the refugee community.

The rationale for providing education is based on the principles enunciated in the 1989 UN convention on the Rights of the Child (Waters and Leblanc, 2005) which states that all children have the right to an education and furthermore, that refugee children have the same rights as any citizens of the country in which they seek asylum. Such a 'rights-based' approach raises important questions about access to schools and quality of educational provision. For example, how can the demand for education be met for the many children from Syria arriving in neighbouring countries where educational resources are already strained (UNHCR, May 2014), or what of the 50 per cent of children between the ages of 6 and 13 who are not enrolled in schools in the Kakuma refugee camp (Steer, 2014) Equivalent figures are unavailable for urban refugees in cities like Bangkok in Thailand or Bogor in Indonesia. Because these populations of refugees are often unregistered, it is impossible to calculate how many children are in fact able to access their right to an education.

Whether in refugee camps or urban settings, education is considered a vital relief service by aid organisations, and by refugees themselves, as a way of providing child protection and psychosocial support, normalising their experiences and building future prospects for individuals as well as communities. There are well-developed, readily accessible plans for delivering education in emergency situations identified by the Inter-agency Network for Education in Emergencies (INEE) an international body of educational professionals working in the field. They have defined 19 minimum standards to promote access to quality education. These standards identify both short-term critical responses and long-term recovery goals. INEE suggests that a rapid educational needs assessment be followed by creation of temporary learning spaces and non-formal education as a 'stopgap'. This stopgap response should be informed by curriculum, which responds to immediate psychosocial as well as learning needs, and works with available teaching staff until more formal arrangements can be put in place (Newby, 2012). The best example of a crisis response is UNICEF's *School in a Box*, (Figure 2.3), which contains the following essential supplies:

> ...exercise books, pencils, erasers and scissors, the kit also includes a wooden teaching clock, wooden cubes for counting, a wind-op/solar radio and a set of three laminated posters (alphabet, multiplication and number tables). The kit is supplied in a locked aluminium box, the lid of which can double as a blackboard when coated with the special paint included in the kit. Using a locally developed teaching guide and curriculum, teachers can establish makeshift classrooms almost anywhere. (UNICEF, March 2013)

Figure 2.3: The school-in-a-box pack issued by UNICEF

Factors that contribute to educational disruption in emergency situations

A case study of Syrian refugees

The ongoing crisis in the Middle East has created increasing waves of refugees from Syria, and now from Iraq as well, as thousands of people flee from civil war and terrorism. The current Syrian refugee experience provides a useful case study of education in an emergency situation. Refugees began fleeing Syria in 2012, but the numbers increased significantly in 2013. The UNHCR now estimates more than 2.8 million have sought protection, with an expected average of 100 00 people arriving each month in 2014 (UNHCR, May 2014).

Syria's education system, like most of its institutions, has collapsed as a result of the civil war with schools closed, buildings destroyed and teachers dispersed. So children arriving in surrounding countries such as Jordan, Lebanon, Egypt and Turkey have already experienced disruptions to their education. However, with the exception of Turkey, there is the advantage of a shared language – Arabic. Even if the spoken dialect differs, a familiar written language ought to provide a measure of continuity. Indeed, whether in or outside camps, all Syrian children are, theoretically, able to go to school in these countries of first asylum. But what seems on the surface to be a situation with good prospects for educational access seems to be failing children both in and out of refugee camps (UNICEF, 2013). The Syrian experience in Jordan illustrates some of the key reasons.

In the Za'atari camp in Jordan, schools are supported by the Jordanian government as well as by a number of aid agencies, and they deliver a curriculum provided by the Jordanian Ministry of Education. However, 76% of girls and 80% of boys between 6 and 18 do not attend school (UNICEF, 2013,). Among the reasons cited in the UNICEF Report: 'Shattered Lives: Challenges and priorities for Syrian children and women in Jordan', are:

- insecurity, poor nutrition, harassment on the way to school, lack of appropriate shoes and clothing, as well as lack of toilet facilities
- conflict between Jordanian teachers and Syrians who, though trained teachers, are only permitted to work as teachers' aides
- children working either inside or outside home
- lack of information about schools and complicated enrolment procedures
- costs of transport

Figure 2.4: Syrian child refugees learn in a makeshift tent classroom in the Kfar Zabad informal tented settlement, in the eastern Bekaa Valley

- overcrowded and poorly resourced schools
- discrimination against Syrians and unacceptable corporal punishment.

As Tran (2013) points out, though the extra demand for teachers in Jordan has been partly addressed by some teacher training, there are still significant questions about quality of teaching. All these factors compound the disincentives to access education and compromise individual children's learning experiences at school.

Access to education in protracted refugee situations

A case study of camps in Thailand

The first refugee camp in Thailand was established along the Thai/ Myanmar border in 1984 to accommodate refugees fleeing from conflict and human rights abuses in Myanmar. The case study of Myanmar refugees in Thailand provides insights into an emergency refugee situation that has become prolonged as conflict in the homeland drags on. The term 'warehousing', with all its negative connotations, is often used to characterise protracted refugee situations in which large populations, like the refugees from Myanmar in Thailand, or the Palestinians in the Middle East, have little hope of repatriation or resettlement and are kept in limbo (Smith, 2004). Within such long-established camps, communities deprived of customary ways of living adapt and develop institutions to suit their circumstances. There are significant consequences for perceptions about the role of education in society as well as for teaching and learning since policy and practice becomes increasingly isolated from either the country of origin or the host community. In protracted refugee situations, with resettlement programs limited, it is difficult for many to find any long-term purpose in education.

Education, both inside Thai refugee camps and in so-called 'learning centres' catering for increasing numbers of migrant workers from Burma, consist of largely unregulated community schools resourced by international NGOs, as well as the local Karen Education Department (KED), which has emerged to fill the vacuum created by the absence of any formal educational authority. KED educational policy and practice is partly a response to the dire conditions in Myanmar especially in ethnic areas. The education system in Myanmar, especially in remote ethnic areas such as Karen State, has been inadequate or non- existent for many years. Brown and Brown (2012) report that:

> Only 1% of the Myanmar national income goes to education. About half young people of secondary school age do not go to school at all. And even now 10% of primary age children are not at primary school.

Figure 2.5: Ban Nai Soi refugee camp in Mai Hong Son, Thailand

Figure 2.6: A classroom in the Mae La Oon Refugee Camp, Thailand

This has created a paradoxical situation: on one hand there are non-formal community schools, both inside and outside the camps, catering for the children of largely illiterate parents, and on the other, there are 'post ten' schools that compete for the brightest students from Myanmar who often make huge personal sacrifices to attend boarding schools hoping to get scholarships to overseas universities. The following account illustrates the priority and value of education for many refugee students.

My education

My name is Thu Yan Aung Adam. I am from Myanmar. My ethnicity is Miek. Since 2001 I and my family arrived to Thailand, at that time I was 11 years old. I didn't go to school when my family was in Myanmar, because my mother was born me in the forest.

I grew up in the forest with my older brother and my mother and father, we all lived together in the forest because we afraid of Burmese solider. I lost my home town and hopeless in the very big forest, I couldn't see the sun very well because many trees were around of me. I worried for my education. I didn't learn nothing I couldn't spell the words correctly and even my name I couldn't write well. I was unhappy when I thought about education I didn't know anything about whether education is good or bad.

After years been in forest, fortunately, my family went to Thailand in a year of 2001, we first arrived in Mae sot, I still remember the first day of my education when I started to learn the ABCD. Among all the children I was the only one who was 11 years old and older than other students, I was not disappointed for my old age and I felt happy with my study. I went to the high school when I was 21 years old. I got the highest marks for the subject of pre-General Education Development (GED) in Boarding High School for Orphans and Helpless (BHSOH).

Thu Yan Aung Adam - Thursday, 23 January 2014, 2:49 PM

A first-hand account of education in a non-formal school

In this section of the chapter, I draw on specific examples to provide a better understanding of what educational experience might be when schooling occurs in a non-formal setting. As pointed out previously, the United Nations has highlighted all children's right to an education. However, a rights-based approach to education raises important questions, not just of access, but also of quality. In situations where refugees have access to formal education, such as in the Middle East, these questions revolve around teacher competence, facilities and inclusion. However, questions about educational quality are even more significant when refugees can only access non-formal education either in refugee camps or in urban areas.

While teachers in Australia are aware that refugee-background students have experienced disrupted schooling, few fully understand the nature of non-formal education. Formal education like that in Australia is a government sponsored, resourced and accredited system with quality controls, a mandated curriculum, qualified teaching staff, and a shared vision of how education contributes to the society's future. Non-formal education has none of these characteristics. In contrast, non-formal schools are community-based establishments, usually in temporary spaces, with few resources and whoever is available from the community to teach, whether trained or untrained. Often schools like 'The New Blood School', the 'Good Morning School', or 'The Peace and Brilliance School' on the Thai/Burma border have evolved from 'stopgap' measures, and have no systematic curriculum, little support from professional educators, and have no formal credentials. Therefore teachers in the Australian situation need to consider assumptions about students' prior learning, and they need to ask questions about what kind of 'school' their students have attended. The following examples illustrate how different 'school' can be.

Recently I visited two community schools in Bangkok set up by Pakistani asylum seekers who were too fearful of disclosure and discrimination to send children to Thai schools, which in any case do not cater for non-Thai speakers. The first, 'The Community Education Center' (Figure 2.7) is housed in three rooms on the fifth floor in a tenement building that had no lift. The rooms were tiny, and classes restricted to 10. The other, the newer 'Hamra School', had two classrooms but no furniture, so children sat on the floor in two crowded classes of 25. Altogether, 105 students attend the school in two shifts, and there is a waiting list of 45. The principal of Hamra confirmed that most students would have had interrupted education with gaps of around a year. There is also a plan to place a playgroup at the back of one room. All the teachers are volunteers and few have teaching qualifications. Figure 2.8 shows a page stuck on a classroom door showing the syllabus for Grade 1.

The Urdu-speaking Pakistanis have no chance of integration in Thailand, therefore there is no incentive to learn Thai. For this reason some schools are bilingual, teaching in Urdu and English, and others only use English as the medium of instruction.

I also met Marwah, a young Palestinian refugee from Syria who speaks French and passable English. Though untrained, she teaches a few children in her house on the outskirts of Bangkok. Some classes are held in Urdu but mostly in English. I asked how decisions were made about curriculum. The answer: 'someone gave me an English textbook but it's too hard for the children so I make up stories and we sing songs'

Figure 2.7: Under 5s in the Kindergarten class writing a letter in the Community Education Center, Bangkok

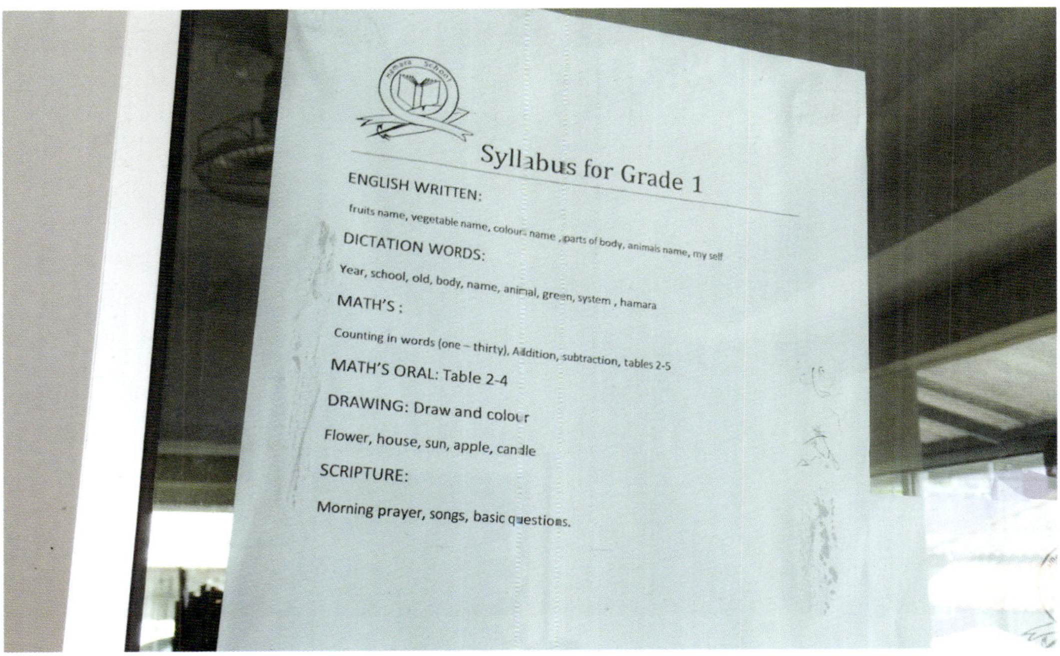

Figure 2.8: Syllabus stuck on the door of Hamra school classroom, Bangkok

(personal communication, January 2014). Given the difficult circumstances faced by this community, such non-formal schools are a remarkable testament to human resilience and determination to provide a future for their children.

In contrast, education for refugees from Myanmar in camps on the Thai border has evolved into a somewhat more stable system, with a network of schools coordinated by the Karen or Karenni education committees. However, as in any kind of schooling, the quality of education is profoundly affected by teacher competence. A focus group of nine teachers from different refugee camps and migrant schools on the Thai border (personal communication, January 2014), confirmed that teacher training is generally very brief – perhaps a couple of weeks or a month, followed up by irregular professional development sessions run by NGOs. In the past, resettlement resulted in a 'brain drain' producing a high turnover of teachers and making recruitment of suitable teachers even more problematic. Figures for 2011 in the Karenni camp showed that only 52 per cent of teachers had themselves achieved education equivalent to Year 10, and that some primary school teachers only achieved Year 6 or 7 (Cranitch & Macfarlane, 2011). According to anecdotal evidence, while languages, maths and social studies are regularly taught, subjects like science, sport, health education or creative arts are rarely taught because teachers lack skills in these areas (Cranitch & Macfarlane, 2011). With large classes, inadequate school buildings, and with resources generally limited to a few textbooks, a chalk board and butcher's paper, as well as poorly trained teachers, there seems to be

Figure 2.9 Teacher Su Meh teaching a class of seven- and eight-year-olds Burmese at a primary school in Ban Nai Soi refugee camp Thailand

little alternative except teacher-directed lessons and rote learning. Indeed, though there is much talk of the need for 'child-centred learning', there is little understanding of what that means and, in practice, without consistent modelling, the default position is to return to rote learning and teacher-directed lessons familiar from Myanmar. Figure 2.9 shows children in one such typical school.

Learning language and literacy in refugee camps on the Thai border

Learners from a refugee background may bring quite different experiences of language learning and literacy practices to the mainstream EAL learners who have attended formal schools. In refugee contexts, since there is little stable sense of the future, decisions about what and how language should be taught and what literacy skills are necessary for adult life are problematic. Consider decisions about the language of instruction in some of the ethnically diverse Thai refugee camps. Schools teach in:

- Karen because they are the ethnic majority in the camp
- Burmese in case of repatriation to Burma
- English because it is a global language, and is thought to provide advantages for resettlement.

This effectively means that children, even as young as five, are expected to learn simultaneously in three languages, and to acquire literacy in three different scripts. For children with the mother tongue Karen, two languages, Burmese and English, are new, but for other ethnic groups such as Mon, Shan or Kachin, all three languages are new. In migrant schools outside the camps, since there is some degree of interaction with the Thai community, Thai language with a different script again is occasionally taught as well, further adding to the language 'soup'.

In practice, the language of instruction varies with teacher competence and available resources. Interviews during an evaluation of Karenni camps in 2011 revealed that some teachers explain concepts from Burmese texts into Karenni, while others use a mixture of Burmese and Karenni, or Karen to translate texts from English. Subject coordinators and head teachers confirmed the ad hoc nature of language choices, and said that many teachers using English textbooks did not understand what they read. Despite acknowledging that such linguistic confusion was unhelpful, camp leaders argued that decisions about languages of instruction were political, rather than educational. (Cranitch & Macfarlane, 2011)

The dominant focus on learning languages does not extend beyond developing more than rudimentary literacy skills, such as reading aloud from a textbook and copying from the blackboard or textbook. There are few texts in the ethnic languages of the camp population. So the initial encounter with literacy is generally through Burmese or English, rather than through mother tongue texts. Burmese textbooks to teach English contain short quite interesting stories, but provide only literal comprehension questions and require no extended oral or written responses. Teachers, lacking confidence in their own English skills save face by concentrating on decoding script and restricting writing to formulaic texts. An example from a member of the focus group (personal communication, January 2014) reflecting on her learning in Myanmar, explained that everyone in her class in primary school was given an essay titled 'Myself' with gaps for the name and date of birth to be copied and submitted for assessment. Literacy rates in the camps are estimated at around 60% (Burma link, 2013), but it is difficult to know what this figure actually reveals about the literacy levels of this 60 per cent, or about the remaining 40 per cent of the population. It is also difficult to know whether literacy development is a product of life in a refugee camp, or of previous educational experiences.

Indeed, one of the most startling revelations that emerged from my experience of five different refugee camps in Thailand was the almost complete absence of text in both public and private spaces.

- Many of the camp inhabitants had come from rural villages with an oral rather than literate tradition.
- Print or digital text are not routinely used except perhaps for religious texts such as the Bible or Koran. Religion whether Buddhist or varieties of Christianity, plays an important role in the community, as an agent of social cohesion.
- There are occasional newspapers from Karen State but no advertisements, and only an occasional sign or billboard to indicate the purpose of a building, or the name of a donor, or to give graphic instructions about the danger of landmines or the need to wash hands.
- Information is passed around by word-of-mouth or camp radio which blares out music and community news.
- Access to paper, computers or internet is limited and there is little if any need to send emails, write letters or create shopping lists. The only books to be found are tattered textbooks or in small donated libraries.
- There are small shops but these are bamboo booths selling household items such as soap or food. The wrapping on any commercial products has writing in Thai, a script that no-one can read.

All this means that the refugee camp communities have developed ways of interacting and communicating that do not involve the kinds of literacy events or practices that are generally assumed as common knowledge.

Another significant observation from my time in the camps relates to the absence of what we would regard as educational 'toys'. I saw games played with balls, small stones, slingshots and rubber bands, but no equipment such as jigsaws, interlocking construction materials or climbing frames that encourage children to develop metacognitive skills such as sorting and classifying as well as fine and gross motor skills through play.

Implications for teachers in Australian classrooms

The key implications for teachers of students from a refugee background arise from the recognition that these students have had vastly different experiences from many other EAL learners. The previous outline of conditions in both emergency and protracted refugee situations contextualises some of the background experiences and expectations that families and students from a refugee background bring to the Australian classroom. The emotional and social impact of refugee experiences does not disappear rapidly or easily. The effects of past trauma on attitudes to learning and classroom behaviour in New Arrivals classrooms are now well documented (Lustig et al., 2004). It is also generally understood that acquiring language for academic purposes takes time (Collier & Thomas, 2009), but for students who have experienced disrupted, informal or poor quality education that may not be age-appropriate, this process takes much longer. These learners need to:

- learn new social conventions and adjust to school routines
- learn a new language and use a new language for learning
- learn about Australian society.

They also need to acquire the peer-appropriate, basic background knowledge assumed in Australian classrooms in relation to specific academic disciplines such as science, mathematics, geography and history. If students are to develop the knowledge and skills required by a mainstream Australian curriculum, they need explicit teaching beyond conventional New Arrival programs. Several studies (including Windle & Miller, 2010; Cranitch, 2010), suggest that, as well as oral English competence, academic literacy and learning skills must be addressed in the long term if students are to succeed in mainstream classes.

Advice to teachers of EAL learners frequently refers to the need to provide a 'text-rich room with a range of extension material and technology' (Miller & Windle, 2010). Most contemporary Australian primary classroom are filled with visual support, with texts stapled to the wall or hanging from the ceiling, and all manner of artefacts to manipulate – an enormous contrast to an austere classroom in tents or bamboo huts which have few educational resources with which to develop metacognitive skills. However, use of concrete materials, educational technology, participating in group work and

Figure 2.10: Cromer public school NSW Students Skype with Japanese counterparts

Figure 2.11: Refugee camp school, Kakuma

problem-solving-based learning may be completely foreign to learners whose prior experience is in teacher-directed classrooms which do not foster independent learning and where 'success' equals repeating information accurately. Learning how to learn in an Australian classroom requires entirely different dispositions, and these need to be taught through careful introduction and repeated modelling. As the photographs (Figures 2.10 and 2.11) highlight, differences between Australian classrooms, and those that students have previously experienced, can be extreme

Research on the importance of explicit teacher scaffolding for EAL learners (Hammond & Gibbons, 2005) demonstrates that carefully sequenced activities, which integrate both curriculum content and language, build both metalinguistic and metacognitive skills. The framework of high challenge, high support involves explicit scaffolding of the goals and purposes for learning as well as the processes.

However, a recent study exploring students' responses to a wordless picture book, highlights the differences between upper primary, recently arrived migrant and refugee-background learners, and the considerable challenges faced by the refugee students (Walsh, Cranitch & Maras, 2012). Unlike the migrant learners who had continuous formal schooling prior to arrival in Australia, the refugee-background learners from Africa, for example, had little or no prior experience of narrative or visual texts. Despite one or more years in a mainstream Australian classroom, these learners had:

- limited book handling skills
- poor prediction skills in the unfolding of a story
- little awareness of the text as an artefact created by an author/illustrator
- difficulty recognising individual images as part of a continuous narrative
- inability to offer meta-textual interpretations or comments about the composition of images.

This study suggested that engaging meaningfully with text, whether print, visual or multimodal, is a long-term process – especially in situations where family literacy practices do not reinforce those of the classroom. It also demonstrated that reading visual images, so often used to support language learning may also require explicit scaffolding.

These findings indicate that teachers need to question assumptions about prior knowledge, skills and learning through observation and research into individual, family and community backgrounds. Students and parents' expectations about school routines, teacher-student relationships, or understandings about activities such as sport or after school care, will almost always be different from what a mainstream teacher might assume. Information about the country of origin, the language and the ethnicity of an individual can provide the basis of powerful support.

However, though teachers have tools for analysis of language learner needs, we lack ways of identifying assets, skills, talents and dispositions which contribute to educational success and good settlement outcomes. Hutchinson and Dorsett (2012, p. 55) suggest that when professionals focus on the background of trauma they tend to overlook individual strengths. They argue that:

> Pathologising the trauma story of refugee people may further alienate refugee people from full inclusion into Australian life by denying their inherent resilience in the face of extraordinary life experiences.

A focus on gaps and deficits tends to overlook the value of students' skills, such as the ability to code switch from different languages, as well as their different kinds of cultural knowledge and understandings based on varied life experiences (Uptin makes similar points in Chapter 3). Building on students' capabilities could constitute positive and powerful assets in the classroom, not just for the individual students, but also for the classroom community as a whole. Some of the ways teachers could do this include:

- recognising that the student who can speak Karen, Burmese and some English has already demonstrated significant language learning skills, and supporting such students to convert this knowledge and skill into 'cultural capital' in the classroom, for example, by encouraging them to teach a word in mother tongue to peers, or to demonstrate a different script
- encouraging learners to maintain their mother tongue by affirming the value of participation in community mother tongue language classes, and by recognising the value of literacy development in the mother tongue for supporting language and literacy development in English
- valuing artistic, musical or sporting ability or recognising personal qualities and life skills builds self-esteem and the resilience required to master the challenges of learning in and through a new language
- integrating aspects of students' culture and language in different curriculum areas, thereby enriching the whole class
- encouraging students to create a portfolio with work samples collected over time to show the students' trajectory of language and learning, chart their progress and celebrate their successes.

This chapter has outlined key features of education in both emergency and protracted refugee settings, in formal and informal schools in order to provide a basis for understanding the kind of experiences learners from refugee backgrounds may bring to the classroom. School is the place where children with a traumatic past can regain their childhood. It is impossible to overestimate the importance of education for successful settlement in Australian society, and the essential role of teachers who provide targeted teaching as well as a supportive classroom climate. Refugees do bring more than they can carry: they contribute talents, skills and energy to the rich diversity that is multicultural Australia.

3

Negotiating a place in Australian schools: Lessons learned from voices of students

Jonnell Uptin

Beginning a new life in a Western democratic society brings with it its own excitements and tensions for all EAL students. Former refugee students who have had a life of disruption and displacement can be excited and, at the same time, overwhelmed at the prospects of beginning school again. Schools play a vital role in this transition, as they are places that teach our children to 'become somebody well' (Wynn, 2007 p. 37). Schools are also the first place where students from refugee backgrounds make connections and establish ways to belong to their new home. However the responsibility to make these connections and to fit in is largely left to the newcomer. In this chapter I seek to address the ways we as teachers can assist in the inclusion process. We need to recognise that refugee students come from diverse backgrounds with differing strengths and needs so that we can better equip these young people for the future. I use the voices of refugee students from recent research to describe the adjustments they have made, what they see as barriers to inclusion and the hopes they possess in navigating a pathway for themselves in their new home.

The background research for this chapter

In writing this chapter I wear two hats, that of a researcher and a teacher. My teaching experience has been diverse – from kindergarten to Year 12 in Australia, Singapore and Thailand. While overseas, I had the opportunity to work alongside many refugees in Northern Thailand teaching Music and English in camps and with organisations assisting in the rehabilitation of young women who had been exploited by the sex trade. This chapter also draws from my PhD research which investigated how young people in Australia who were formerly refugees negotiate their cultural identity, creating new narratives for themselves that accommodate the complexity of the past, the present and the future. There were twelve participants in this narrative enquiry aged from 16 to 20 years. They described themselves as originating from Karenni and Chin States of Burma, from Myanmar, also Burundi, Southern Sudan, Democratic Republic of Congo, Sierra Leone, and Togo, however, the participants spent most of their lives in the host countries of Thailand, Malaysia, Kenya, Zambia, Benin, South Africa and Ghana. Interviews and focus groups were used to collect the data. Some of the participants came to Australia with their family and others with adults from their tribe. The study found that 'school was the place where the participants talked of wanting to belong, of trying to belong, each talked of the high value education had in their own family and culture, and this meant they placed a high price on succeeding socially and academically' (Uptin, Wright & Harwood, 2013 p. 126).

Recognising the diversity of former refugee students

Discussing refugee students as if they were a whole homogenous group is problematic, as few generalisations can be made. Even more problematic is the way in which we discuss former refugee students. By discussing and therefore viewing former refugee students as a group that is 'at risk' it is easy to lose sight of the individual student and not recognise what these resilient young people have already accomplished. Those who have worked alongside refugee students encounter great diversity amongst this student population. This diversity not only consists of language and ethnic background but also in more complex issues that emerge when you ask questions such as: How long has the child lived in displacement? Was the host country hostile or welcoming to refugees? Did they live in a camp or in urban areas? Was schooling makeshift or formal? Were their teachers trained? Did they experience war? Have they left behind significant people in their lives? All of these factors and many more affect how students transition into school life. Table 3.1 presents some of the participants from my PhD study and looks at three factors that can potentially affect refugee learners. This gives an insight into the complexity of each individual circumstance.

As Table 3.1 shows refugee students are a diverse group. Not all have had disrupted schooling as seen in the case of Hannah, Gabriella and Peta, but others have had a most

Table 3.1: The complexity of refugee learner backgrounds

Name* Nationality	Schooling before Australia	Dislocation factors	Disruption to family
Gabriella Congolese	Private English-speaking school in South Africa for 7 years Speaks 3 languages	Escaped Democratic Republic of Congo with her family before war broke out; Father was an engineer Lived in South Africa in an urban area	Settled in Australia with parents and 8 brother and sisters
Hannah Sierra Leonean	Began school in a refugee camp school in Ghana Moved to a private English-speaking school in Accra. Speaks 4 languages.	Escaped Sierra Leone with mother and father Lived in refugee camp in Guinea for 1 year then a refugee camp in Ghana for 3 years Moved to Accra where her father worked as hotel manager	Witnessed death of her extended family in war in Sierra Leone Witnessed starvation of her Aunt in camp Mother kidnapped from camp in Ghana Came to Australia alone with her father.
Joseph Sudanese	Studied in the Kakuma refugee camp school, administered by the UNHCR and partners Speaks 2 languages.	Walked through Sudan to Kenya with older brother. Stayed in Kakuma refugee camp.	Lost his mother and father in the war in Sudan. Lived with his father's second wife in Kakuma refugee camp When he came to Australia he found that his mother was living in Kenya and father in Sudan. He has not as yet visited them.
Sing Me Karenni	Attended a makeshift school where she was taught Karenni culture and language by elders in the camp Speaks 2 languages	Arrived at the border camp in Thailand at the age of one; Had never been outside the camp until leaving to come to Australia	Came to Australia with parents and 4 siblings
Jai Burmese	On the Thai/Burmese border Jai and his friends made their own school where they taught each other what they knew Upon converting to Christianity Jai was admitted to a makeshift Christian school in Mae Sot	Jai, his brother and mother walked into Thailand when he was 8 years old. Jai's mother found work in a factory Both boys were boarders at the Christian school but this did not stop the Thai police forcing the students to work at building roads.	Came to Australia with mother and brother; Has lost contact with his father
Peta Burundian	Schooled in an English-speaking private school in Zambia	Escaped with her family to Congo and then to Zambia when she was a baby; Lived in Zambia for 13 years where her mother and father ran a corner shop	Came to Australia with mother, father and 2 sisters.

** All names have been changed to protect the privacy of participants in the study* deprived schooling experience, as in the case of Sing Me and Jai. Not all experienced the trauma of war but others have suffered extreme loss like Hannah and Joseph. Some endured the banal monotony of refugee camps, never seeing or moving in the outside world like Sing Me, while others survived on the streets like Jai.

Additionally, we cannot confine some of these students to an 'at-risk' category. In fact the schooling experience of Hannah, Gabriella and Peta was a productive one. Gabriella and Peta came to Australia with their families intact, having grown up in relatively peaceful countries as urban refugees. Placing the deficit label of 'at risk' upon such students can hinder their progress in school. In recognising this diversity within the refugee student population we can devise strategies to meet the individual learning needs of the each student. Gabriella is a good example of this:

> Gabriella escaped war with her family largely intact. She does not fit with the 'traumatised refugee' label. Her father was able to work in South Africa and prioritised their finances by sending his children to a good private school, resisting the label often given to refugees as 'helpless victim'. However, when Gabriella arrived in high school in Australia she was automatically placed in the bottom classes. After coming first in Maths and English she asked the teachers to move her up to the intermediate level. This did not happen so Gabriella knocked on the principal's door. She told me in her interview that she presented herself to the principal as a South African migrant showing the principal photos of her old school and the awards she had won: she was resisting the label of 'at risk'. After the meeting the principal stepped in and moved her up two levels to a more advanced class.

Lessons learned

Understanding the complex diversity in former refugee students' backgrounds has enabled me as a teacher to adjust and accommodate to the individual needs of each EAL student. Learning from Gabriella's experience, it can be seen that the teachers in her school focused more on the deficit model of 'refugee' than the results in her tests. Impressively, Gabriella invented a new discourse for herself, moving away from the 'traumatised, victim' and 'at risk' labelling of refugees. She chose a new way to represent herself to her principal and it gave her freedom for upward mobility and consequently a higher standard of education. Unfortunately other students may not possess such social intelligence. Therefore, as Cranitch argues in Chapter 2, it becomes even more important that teachers recognise the diversity in the refugee student population and make efforts to learn about their students' backgrounds.

Finding out about a student's background can be a long process. I am not advocating invading the student's private life, but there are ways that teachers can find out some aspects of their students' backgrounds. An understanding of what students have survived might well assist teachers to put into place the skills and steps the student needs to progress and transition into their new home.

As a teacher I used the following ways to learn about my students' backgrounds:

- asked questions like – What languages do you speak? Where did you learn that language? Who taught it to you? What did your classroom look like?
- googled the name of the school or the refugee camp
- watched movies and YouTube clips of the region
- asked to watch the students' favourite songs on YouTube
- asked students to bring in photos of family
- 'buddied' the student with another student from their own language background
- found community support structures with people who speak the students' language
- talked with members of the students' ethnic community
- talked with multicultural liaison officer to get access to information.

A note of caution

While recruiting young former refugees for my PhD research, I found that there was a lot of fear around being formally interviewed. A trusted Sudanese elder, on enquiry, disclosed that most refugee families have undergone multiple interviews by authorities to determine refugee status, and depending upon how 'well' it goes, the interview can determine who gets to resettle in another country. Children are often interviewed separately and if there are discrepancies in the family members' stories the whole family can lose their chance for resettlement. Therefore, be aware that direct questioning can feel like an inquisition again to many refugee students, causing them to close down and remain quiet. It is only when they understand that they are safe will the students open up.

Students have been found to tell complete fabrications of their past life. They might do this because the past is too traumatic to face or because they want to escape deficit refugee labelling that can disempower them. Whatever the reasoning, my experience has been that students later admit to the fabrications, expressing the realisation that they are now safe and want to tell their real story.

Making the adjustment to school in Australia

For those young people in the research who had spent many years in a refugee camp, living life as a 'citizen' was a new and daunting experience. Some of the participants described missing out on the everyday things in life that prepare children as a citizen. When camps become protracted containment areas that keep refugees in, young people miss out on a myriad of experiences that other people take for granted. It is more than a gap in school ***it is a gap in life.***

Sing Me talks of the first time she and her family went to the supermarket:

> First time we shopping very scary, so many shops. We go to shops and think they take our money and give us food, like in camp. No, this not the way. We go to supermarket, at the door is like police [security guard] we think he will not let us in but we need food so we try and he let us. We watch other people [in the supermarket] and they take thing [she mimes people taking off the shelf], you know and put it in basket. We very scared, think the police will come just like Thai police. Thai police see refugee and put in jail. We think police will put us in jail. I watch other people I think maybe I can go. I can go. So I go and look at food and put in basket, no one do [anything]. We give all our money to lady. She not angry. She give me back some money then we go home, no police come, very good.

Other participants, like Phi Lo talked of his excitement of riding in a car for the first time, Another student told of her sister discovering how to flush a toilet at Sydney airport and showing the rest of the family what to do. Most spoke of learning how to swim, ride a bike, use a computer, a phone, and of writing in a book for the first time. Jai spoke of sitting in class and being given a book to read, he said that he wanted to look smart so he opened it and pretended to read then the teacher came and turned the book the right way up. One student worried about what general knowledge she didn't know, 'like who Hitler was'. She also worried that she did not have a clue as to what she didn't know and this made it impossible for her to use her own initiative to catch up. Thus 'catching up' consisted of much more than literacy and numeracy skills.

This 'lack of knowing' was not just concerned with encountering the new but was also about re-interpreting what they had previously understood. The Burmese young people spoke of their fear of strangers, they told how as refugees they would not look up when they walked in the streets, but in Australia, as they walk around the streets, people say 'hello' and shop keepers will talk freely to them. Adjusting to such changes in relating to others takes time and a lot of personal energy.

Overall the participants saw the potential to be 'someone' other than 'a refugee,' but talked about being overwhelmed by the multiple steps needed to move toward becoming 'someone'.

Negative responses to school

However not all changes were viewed as positive. Some of the participants in the study spoke of the confinement of school, of having to wear a uniform, being made to attend every day, and of getting in trouble for not being on time. Some of the boys talked of hating bells and of only being able to eat when the bell rang. This confounded them when there was so much food anyway. Other stories showed how the complexity of home life affected school life. For example, another student, regularly had to move between her mother's and auntie's home and talked of deciding not to go to school if she forgot her socks. She explained:

> *If I go to school with the wrong socks I just get a big headache from every teacher. They think I don't care about my education, but really, I just forget my socks.*

Lessons learned

The above examples emphasise that for some former refugee students the adjustment they must make to live and learn in Australian society affects all parts of their social, cognitive and physical life. The transition of coming from some of the poorest regions of the world to one of the richest countries in the world is often navigated alone.

My first approach to this as a teacher was to:

- create an environment where students were encouraged to consider that no question was a stupid question
- begin units of work with brainstorming what we know and what we want to know, making sure that the discussion is supported by pictures and hands-on activities
- create spaces where open conversations between students can occur and where peer 'teaching' can occur so that everyday knowledge can be shared
- establish a buddy system where students who had been in school longer were encouraged to support newly arrived students (Gibbons, 1991)
- build class mind maps so students can see the multiple connections among ideas
- be prepared to stop and fill in the missing gaps, scaffolding the content from the known to the unknown
- tell stories.

Language learning is also culture learning

Cultural transition for many refugee and EAL students from developing countries is often overlooked in teaching, and the impact of this is often underestimated. Learning culture, learning new ways of living, new ideas and the mainstream values in a new land can be overwhelming for refugee students. Often the student faces this type of learning alone. In the classroom, the concentration on academic language and literacy development is justified, yet the skill of learning culturally appropriate conversational registers (that is when to speak, or how to speak or how to behave) is often left to the student to learn as they progress through school.

Learning Australian cultural ways was a great concern to the participants in the study because the cultural expectations were not fully explained. Many of the students expressed the frustration of not knowing until it was too late what they needed to do to achieve in life. For example, Joseph spoke of 'a big mistake' he made when trying to get a part-time job.

> *All the pieces of paper you get at school, you know the certificates and the merits and that, well he [potential boss] wanted them. I'm like, I just thought they were paper.*

The role of the teacher was at times confusing to the participants. Gabriella talked of viewing the teacher as an extended parent in the Democratic Republic of Congo and how she missed the warmth and sense of belonging that this close relationship brought to her learning. Hannah described how relieved she was when she found out a teacher could not hit her, but she also described how difficult it was to find out if the teacher was pleased with her.

The concept that teachers cannot hug or hit a student can leave the student confused as to how behaviour is assessed and monitored. In Australia the importance of talking to a student about behaviours and the giving of merits and demerits is the cultural norm. However I suggest that explaining these differences in discipline could assist students to smoother transitions.

Lessons learned

Having spent more than fifteen years teaching in schools I am aware that teaching culture to EAL students is often seen as part of the 'hidden curriculum' and is ad hoc and incidental and often occurs only when the student is in trouble. The concern here is that if a student cannot pick up on the cultural nuances of relating to people within the Australian context then value judgements about that student can easily and quickly be formed. Linguistic mistakes are often expected from EAL and former refugee students and correction often follows. However if a student makes a cultural impropriety it can be easily assumed that the student is behaving rudely. When students get culture wrong it sends a very different message to what might have been intended by the student, and this isolates new students from the mainstream culture of the school.

The implications of not teaching cultural norms can be seen in the following drawn from my personal experience as an EAL teacher.

> The talk from some teachers regarding the Sudanese students began to change. Previously these teachers were happy with the improvement in the English acquisition but then I began to hear comments such as 'I can't warm to that kid', 'I just can t trust him', 'She's sneaky', creeping into the conversation.
>
> After spending time reflecting upon what was happening I changed my teaching and I also informed the staff of Sudanese cultural norms.
>
> In my EAL lessons I explained the Australian cultural norm, the 'Look me in the eye when you are talking to me' rule I also talked to the students about what looking in the eye demonstrates: it shows respect, consideration and honesty. Discussions with the students arose about their own cultural perceptions of this action. We played staring games, role played talking to teachers and shop keepers until the students developed an 'Australian way of talking'.
>
> I emphasised that now the students had two ways of talking to people, 'a school way of talking' and a 'home way of talking' and that both are valuable because both show respect and care.

What motivated my teaching in this area was listening to conversations with refugee students and hearing their desire to make significant connections in Australian society. I found that there were two assumptions that I could NOT make as a teacher:

1 My students would automatically pick up on some of the fundamental 'rules of engagement' that exist in Australian society.

2 Others (like the teachers of the Sudanese students), would understand that ways of relating can be vastly different in cultures.

It was up to me as their teacher to explicitly teach the cultural norms of their new home and not doing this could disadvantage the student. In explicitly teaching cultural practices I tried to:

- make sure to frame the conversation around discussions of difference, rather than deficit, and avoid words like 'right and wrong', 'correct and incorrect'
- clarify that students can choose to use these different ways of meaning and behaving
- allow for time and conversations with students around sharing how each other's culture demonstrates values such as respect, friendship and behaving as a 'good student'
- be prepared to laugh about the way Australians do things.

This way of teaching breaks down the mystery and confusion that EAL students often experience. By addressing the subtle differences between 'home culture' and 'school culture' we can open up new conversations about cultural similarities as well. It also gives EAL students the tools and framework to understand how to navigate their own transition. The conversations that develop from this teaching can also teach Australian-born students of other ways to view the world and can foster understanding and inclusivity. Whether students choose to employ these practices is not our concern, because many of these practices can be closely tied to how the student constructs their identity. However our responsibility as an educator is to ensure they know what is available to choose from.

Negotiating between cultures

One of the issues explored in the research project was the idea of living in and between two cultures. However, an added complexity here is that many refugee students, due to being displaced, have lived in multiple countries. Many had left their home country as a small child or were born in a third country, for example, Peta's family left Burundi to escape the genocide in Rwanda. Peta was born in the Democratic Republic of Congo and they then moved to Zambia where she spent primary and middle school life. Although on her passport Peta is seen as Burundian she has never been there and she sees herself as Zambian. Now in the safety of Australia, Peta's parents have joined the Burundian diaspora and they identify strongly with Burundi as home. Peta, however, identifies strongly with the happy-go lucky Zambian. Many former refugee students have had a lot of practice at negotiating between cultures and performing 'at home' and 'in society' identities. This is not to say these negotiations are easy as many of the participants spoke of being tired of endlessly adjusting to different contexts.

Nevertheless all participants talked of a 'home culture' that was vastly different from 'school culture'. The stories told by the participants were of negotiating between home and school culture to gain the most benefit from both places. Home was seen as their comfort, connecting them to their past but school was seen as the promise of a brighter future. They all spoke of investing a huge amount of energy into establishing connections with school and of taking up the practices that would assist them to be seen as 'good students'. The young women from African countries spoke of traversing gender barriers as well. Here Gabriella speaks of home:

> But even my own family – we are taught that men are still superior. They are more intelligent, their opinion, it should be highly valued although they say nonsense or they are wrong . . . For me I'm a bit stubborn. I'd say I would always go sideways, maybe I was born strange. There was so much things that happened around me as soon as I stepped here [in Australia] I believed in equalarianism. Is that right? I believe everyone is equal. So it's funny you know, like at home I am a part of the family and my father and brothers speak and I put my head down. But in the morning, I put on my school uniform and I look in the mirror and I put my shoulders back and my head up and I say in the mirror 'I am an Australian woman'. I go to school like that'.

As Gabriella negotiates her life across different cultural domains she describes how she complies with the status quo at home but as she goes to school she embodies the young Australian woman ready to take full benefit of her educational opportunities.

Lessons learned

Areas around gender expectations can be particularly sensitive, yet I have seen teachers deal with issues with equal sensitivity. Getting to know the parents, particularly fathers, can be valuable in assisting students with navigating the different expectations from home and school. Many parents from refugee backgrounds highly respect the position of their child's teacher. I have called upon this elevated position, by approaching the father first, explaining the activity and how this can benefit the family – it can become a win-win situation.

Resisting the label of 'refugee' to establish belonging

Importantly, this research found that the young people in the study desired to make authentic connections in Australian society. However each participant had been confronted with being positioned as an 'outsider' in their new homeland. As the political discourse surrounding 'the refugee' has heightened suspicion and polarised attitudes toward refugees in Australia (Hattam & Every, 2010; Keddie, 2011) negotiating how to belong in Australian society has become more difficult for former refugees. Having lived fractured childhoods the young people expressed a longing to find home and be at home in their surroundings. One of the barriers to this was the deficit 'refugee' label. Much of the discussion with the young participants centred on how they could reposition their identity. This was of particular concern to Gabriella as she was preparing to enter university at the time of data collection. She states:

> Once an African refugee, always a refugee. The reason is that label, that title, doesn't go away for people with black skin. 'Cause many people, if you look at that part of the world, even when you look at ads of refugees, they mostly have African faces. They kind of symbolise suffering and many people they come with that image and they don't get away from the word 'refugee'.
>
> I have my friends from Serbia and all those countries, for goodness sake, as soon as they've entered here they've landed in straight away. No one ever calls them 'refugee' again. But people, even I'm five years in Australia, some people I know are here for 10 years and they still hear the word 'refugee'. And they even accept it. That's the problem. ... It's a different story for us and people still call us refugee and we are here with Australian citizenship. I don't understand that concept.

Here Gabriella resists the equation that being African equals refugee. She also resists the idea that being a refugee means she is a victim, and she resists this positioning by society. Hannah describes how innocent conversations can make her feel isolated:

> Although I have been here for 5 years I still get people calling out asking, you know, when I go buy a coffee, 'Where are you from?' I say, 'I come from here'. 'Do you like it here?' they say.
>
> I've been here for 5 years and they still ask you that question and that reminds you that you don't belong. You stand out everywhere you go. If I had the same skin colour as everybody else I would go and order coffee like everybody else. So I feel –ah. Then they ask, 'How long are you here for?' and that is the question that reminds me that I can't belong. Because somebody is always telling me that at the end of this I will pack my bags and leave. If someone says, how long are you here for, it means I can never just relax and BE here.

Because of physical difference, students can be viewed as 'outsiders' by some and thus cannot relax and be 'at home,' which can disrupt authentic connections to their new home in Australia. Joseph too talks of the ways in which he sees that he is framed as different in Australian society. He suspects the demands upon him are due to a type of indirect racism.

> I keep hearing the word 'integrate, you must integrate.' Integrate, what does that mean? So I ask and they tell us, they say 'go to school' so I go to school, I integrate.
>
> Then they say 'get a house,' we got a house, we integrate. Then they say 'get a car,' we got a car, then they say, 'join a club,' I play basketball but still I hear 'integrate, you must integrate.'
>
> I think, 'What do you want me to do? Peel off my skin? Maybe then I integrate'.

Many refugee and EAL students come to learn that Australian society has elements that are racist. Schools can be and should be places that work hard to debunk the myths around 'white Australia'.

Focusing on strengths

Overwhelmingly what was evident in the young people who participated in the research was their capacity to hope. They told of the ways they had persisted, refusing to give in. Each talked of their present frustrations in the light of their past and concluded that 'today is better than yesterday' (Jacqueline). As with other research (Ramirez & Matthews, 2008; Gifford et al., 2009), the young people showed unbounding energy toward the new tasks that were set before them, they had hope that they would succeed. They had lived long enough in Australia to understand how hard they needed to work in order to achieve their goals. In some cases they had adjusted their goals to more realistic expectations for their future. Additionally the young people had an ability to see their present circumstance through the lens of the past and this was a source of hope as well.

The participants cited numerous instances where school had contributed to a sense of belonging. As with (Gifford et al., 2009) being seen as a learner and a contributor to the learning culture of a school was very important to the participants. Some told of how teachers had allowed them to express this hope through telling their stories in writing, drama, art and in composing songs. After this the participants told of making new friendships with students in the class and of being invited to social events. The Burmese students who had lived in camps found that the school garden was a place where they could contribute and even introduce their own herbs and vegetables, teaching other students how to cook with them.

Feeling safe at school was acknowledged as a priority by the young people. Safety was measured by how often teachers smiled, whether the teacher listened to them, and how they made jokes with the students. Another sign of safety for the students was that the school had places that were beautiful to which they contributed by painting murals on walls and helping tend the gardens.

Lessons learned

Being involved in music, sport and art projects with former refugee students both in Thailand and Australia I have observed the resourcefulness and resilience of many refugee students. The need to have fun was an important element for the students both in my experience with teaching and in the research project, yet they did not ask to be entertained. The students possessed an ability to make their own fun: they brought humour to the most menial of tasks; they initiated jokes and games; and they found delight in the smallest of things. For the African students joy was displayed in exuberant ways such as high fiving each other, hugging and doing a spontaneous dance. For the Burmese students it was a witty comment, giggling and telling a funny story. As a teacher I relished those times they taught me to live in and enjoy the moment and simply appreciate being alive.

As teachers, we need to create classrooms that acknowledge the identities and strengths of former refugee students, and we need to recognise that these young people are survivors and have already demonstrated incredible resilience in life.

Conclusion

Students from refugee backgrounds can be the most vulnerable of our student population. Working to give these students the skills, attitudes and values they need to participate and contribute to our society can be confounding and at the same time very rewarding. What makes teaching former refugee students less confounding is challenging the stereotypes and seeing the diversity within the refugee student population. When we learn more of each student's background and the quality of schooling they received we can concentrate on the individual student with their strengths and needs. In this chapter I have as much as possible included the voices of former refugee youths telling their stories. Even within this small group we can see the diversity of educational experience before their arrival in Australia, the diversity of tragedy they encountered as refugees, their different strengths and interests that are developing and the complexity of their needs.

The skills that former refugee students need to function in Australian life go far beyond knowledge of English language, literacy and numeracy (important though these are). As seen in this chapter they extend to having opportunities to engage in life experiences. Extracurricular activities can therefore become a significant joy and learning experience to former refugee students. Not all students' responses to school life were positive. Some found some of the practices of school confining and restrictive. However, explicit teaching of what is considered as 'normal' cultural ways in Australian society can help here. By giving students these insights, they can then have the power to choose to take up these practices.

Negotiating the differences between home and school cultures can result in reconstructing a school identity and a home identity in order to keep all connections strong. Unfortunately, as seen in the young people's stories, no matter how hard one person may work to be included this must be reciprocated with acceptance. With the current political discourse that positions refugees as outsiders, teachers need to be aware that former refugee students can be particularly vulnerable to the pain of exclusion, yet again. Schools, now more than ever, need to actively work to create safe cultural places for all students.

Schools can actively create inclusion by recognising the strengths and hope that individual young former refugees bring to school. When we simply characterise the refugee student as 'at risk', we silence 'the extraordinary childhoods of refugee children and youth' (Christie & Sidhu 2002, p. 289). This chapter has been framed by including the lessons I have learned in teaching refugee students and therefore I leave you with one final thought. Rather than seeing former refugee students as 'at risk', 'victim' or 'traumatised', like Hayward et al. (2008) I see them as 'normal people who are forced to deal with abnormal and traumatic situations' (p. 81).

4

Working with at-risk EAL students in non-metropolitan primary classrooms

Jacqueline Coleman

The focus of this chapter is on teacher practices in non-metropolitan classrooms with recently arrived refugee students, where a single, mainstream teacher may be solely responsible for the education of EAL students throughout one school year. Until recently, the majority of refugees and immigrants to Australia have settled in large capital cities. However, as recent figures from the Australian Bureau of Statistics (ABS) demonstrate, an increasing number of refugees and immigrants are now settling outside metropolitan areas (ABS, 2013). Consequently, more at-risk EAL students, including those from refugee backgrounds and/or those with minimal or disrupted schooling, prior to arriving in Australia, are now enrolling in schools that have previously had little experience with such students. This change to the student body presents significant challenges to mainstream teachers accustomed to teaching relatively culturally and linguistically homogenous classes. They must attempt to integrate their new EAL students into their classes, and meet their specific learning needs, often with little, if any, systemic professional learning support. Research in similar contexts in the United States has shown that teachers may feel inadequately prepared to meet these challenges and find having EAL students in their classes a 'burden' (Valdes, 2001) or 'overwhelming' (Walker, Shafer & Iiams, 2004).

The chapter begins by addressing the types of evidence-based pedagogies available to inform teacher practice with at-risk EAL students. It then discusses a small-scale research study carried out in two primary schools in non-metropolitan New South Wales in classrooms in which refugee at-risk EAL students were enrolled and considers the implications of the study's findings for teachers and their students.

Evidence-based pedagogical practices available to teachers

Freeman and Freeman (2007) conducted a review of Second Language Acquisition (SLA) research, and of research into effective educational programs internationally. Based on the findings of this review, they contend that there is 'widespread agreement on the principles that underlie successful programs' for EAL students (Freeman & Freeman, 2007, p. 349). To support EAL students toward academic success teachers need to:

- engage students in challenging and theme-based curriculum to foster the development of academic concepts
- draw on students' cultural, linguistic and background experiences
- organise collaborative activities and scaffold instruction
- create students who are confident and value school and themselves as learners.

These principles are appropriate for all students and are especially important for at-risk students. To feel confident and to benefit academically from successful programs, students must first feel safe. Teacher practices which provide social support, or 'pastoral' care to these students, where 'pastoral' care is understood as attention to the psychosocial and material needs of students (Konu & Rimplea, 2002), are crucial first steps toward the first three more broadly 'pedagogical' principles suggested by Freeman and Freeman. Social support for EAL students may include practices such as affirmative comments and gestures and positive reinforcement for achievement and effort.

However, 'pastoral' social support alone is insufficient to foster the academic success of EAL students. Foucault (1983) discusses pastoral care in terms of 'pastoral power'. He claims that all pastoral relationships potentially position those who receive pastoral care as being in some way deficient and in need of behaviour modification. If EAL students are positioned principally as recipients of pastoral care, teachers may unconsciously limit the students' access to the 'field of action' of academic achievement. For this reason it is imperative that teachers move beyond pastoral practices with at-risk EAL students and into the implementation of evidence-based pedagogical practices which align with Freeman and Freeman's first three principles and which position these students as students who can achieve academically.

Key to the implementation of appropriate practices is the inclusion of EAL students in all curricular activities (Cummins & Early, 2011). Nonetheless, inclusion alone will not guarantee meaningful learning of curriculum content for EAL students, 'no matter how friendly, egalitarian and caring the environment' of their classrooms (Gibbons, 2002, p. 59). Student access to the curriculum is facilitated by teachers who view inclusion as the foundation for implementing practices which indicate to their EAL students that they hold high academic expectations for them and which also provide them with the instruction and experiences needed to meet these expectations. The following section looks at practical ways in which the principles of Freeman and Freeman (2007) may be applied in mainstream classes which include at-risk EAL students.

High expectations and practices to support achievement

Research shows the powerful effect of a combination of high expectations for students and pedagogies based on developing transferable, deep learning practices (Coady, et al., 2008; Newmann & Associates, 1996). High expectations, derived from a belief that all students can achieve, are demonstrated when students are asked to work a little beyond their current academic level, and when they are 'scaffolded' to do so. Scaffolding for EAL students should include as per Walqui (2006, p. 159):

> both structure and process, weaving together several levels of pedagogical support, from macro level planning of curricula over time to micro-level moment-to-moment scaffolding and the contingent variation of support responsive to interactions as they unfold.

For primary teachers who are responsible for the education of EAL students across all curriculum areas, it is necessary to engage in both the 'macro level' of careful cross-curricular planning and 'moment-to-moment' scaffolding in order to realise high expectations (Hammond & Gibbons, 2005; van Lier, 1996). Part of the 'macro level' of scaffolding is the provision of quality criteria for the work students are required to produce. Quality criteria should be explicit, and especially for EAL students, have a clear focus on the language to be used. Skills and knowledge to meet these criteria should be taught in context within carefully planned activities across all curriculum areas.

Practices to develop higher order thinking and extended oral participation

Higher order thinking skills are mental processes involving the analysis, synthesis, evaluation and application of knowledge. The development of these skills is crucial to EAL students' school success. They are actively constructed through extended language use by students and teachers in meaningful interactions focused on subject content. Extended classroom use of language is often termed 'Substantive' communication (NSW DET, 2003). It is particularly important for the development of higher order thinking due to the modelling of academic language and of 'thinking aloud' that it provides for EAL students. Extended oral participation thus contributes to the development of both academic language and metacognitive strategies because it provides opportunities to hear and produce increasingly academic spoken English (which forms a bridge into written academic language) and to receive feedback on their language use in a supportive environment.

The 'comprehensible output' hypothesis (Swain, 2000) claims that the act of 'producing' in a target language, English in the case of EAL students, is essential to language learning. By producing language (either spoken or written) in a class activity, an EAL student can receive feedback on his/her performance from teachers and peers. Interacting during activities with their peers provides a meaningful context for language use as well as a source of strong motivation for EAL students to improve their English proficiency. They also provide feedback or 'moment-to-moment contingent variation of support responsive to interactions as they unfold' (Walqui, 2006, p. 159). Feedback which takes the form of explicit teaching of grammar in context, for example, can assist the learner to notice language form in relation to meaning, and thus to build greater accuracy in language use. Language-focused learning conversations, including shared metalanguage used by both teachers and students, contribute to learner internalisation of improved form and accuracy, and thus increase the academic language proficiency of students.

Practices which link learning to students' outside school knowledge

In addition to extended oral participation, it is important to draw on students' cultural, linguistic and background experiences (Freeman & Freeman, 2007). Utilising EAL students' cultural knowledge and language has been shown to increase minority students' engagement with academic concepts and thus their academic outcomes (Nieto & Bode, 2008). It allows the students' identities to become part of classroom practices. Specifically, there is significant evidence of the positive impact on the English literacy proficiency of EAL students where strategic use is made of their first languages (L1s) in classrooms (Cummins & Early, 2011). Using EAL students' L1s can engage them with cognitively challenging material beyond their present level of English proficiency. Producing and displaying curriculum content-related texts by EAL students in their L1s has also been proven to facilitate the process of engagement.

Two case studies

The purpose

In most primary schools, the class teacher is responsible for teaching students across all curriculum areas. With the increasing enrolment of EAL students in non-metropolitan primary schools, the purpose of the study described here was to gain a picture of the types of practices being employed by mainstream teachers of these students in non-metropolitan areas, and of how these might relate to the students' academic attainment.

The region

Historically, the region in which the study took place has had very low levels of cultural diversity with only 12.5 per cent of the population being born overseas and the majority of these in English-speaking countries (ABS, 2013). School One is located in the biggest city in this region, which has a population of approximately 150 000 (ABS, 2013). The school is situated in a lower socioeconomic area of the city, and despite the lack of diversity in the region as a whole, is highly multicultural with children of 27 nationalities. It has seen the arrival of successive waves of immigrants and refugees, due to the relatively low cost accommodation available in the surrounding area. In contrast, School Two is located in an upper middle class, predominantly Anglo-Australian area in the same regional city as School One. There is much less cultural diversity and many of those students from diverse backgrounds are children of visiting professionals working on contracts at the nearby teaching hospital and university.

Two Year 3 teachers took part in the study. Both are female English monolinguals and both have had more than twenty years of experience teaching in mainstream primary classes. The teacher at School One had approximately 15 years of experience teaching EAL students, including some refugee students, whereas the teacher at School Two had no previous experience with refugee students. Like many teachers in non-metropolitan areas in Australia, neither had formal EAL qualifications. In both classes there were three at-risk EAL students of refugee background – two girls and one boy (a total of six students). All were aged eight or nine and had been born in Sudan and had come to Australia as infants with their families. All six children were classified as students whose understanding and production of spoken and written English was limited to a range of familiar social and educational situations (sometimes called 'Phase Two Learners').

Listening to the teachers

Before moving on to focus on the pedagogical practices observed during the study, it is important to hear the teachers' perspectives with regard to their teaching contexts and their at-risk EAL students. In interviews during the study both teachers said that they had received inadequate professional learning support. This meant that they had not had opportunities to learn about, and develop proficiency in evidence-based pedagogies aligned with Freeman and Freeman's principles, to help them to meet the challenge of teaching EAL students in their mainstream classrooms. The teacher at School Two, who had never taught at-risk EAL students prior to those enrolled at the time of the study, had received no professional learning at all to support her in meeting this significant challenge. The teacher at School One described having attended only *'a couple of one day sessions, but they were quite a few years ago – so not very current.'* Despite this lack of systemic provision of professional learning to support them, both teachers clearly identified the central learning need of their at-risk EAL students as being English language development: *'... what pulls them up sometimes is the language'* (Teacher at School Two). They also recognised that conversational fluency did not indicate proficiency in the academic language required for school success, making comments such as the following: *'Conversational English comes a lot easier ... quicker'* (Teacher at School Two); and *'applying it [knowledge of Conversational English] then even to write a sentence, to construct a sentence is a lot harder for them'* (Teacher at School One).

However, enacting pedagogies to bridge children from conversational English to academic English across the curriculum, without appropriate professional learning is extremely challenging. Perhaps not surprisingly, both teachers in the study stated frankly that they felt unable to meet the learning needs of their EAL students in their mainstream classes. As well as lack of professional learning support, the teacher at School Two identified competing priorities of different students, or *'so many different needs'* of other non-EAL students with their *'own little set of problems'* as contributing to this challenging and complex situation.

Both teachers demonstrated positive, caring attitudes toward their EAL students, and appreciation of the challenges students faced learning in English and of their efforts within the classroom. For example, when describing the various children in her class, the teacher at School Two said of her EAL students, *They're not my three who don't appear to listen and understand. Those are three who do and maybe they've had to work harder at it* .... The teacher at School One expressed a similarly positive attitude and appreciation of her EAL students when she contended that, ... *if some of these kids* [English speaking background children in the class] *had had to cope with what they're coping with they wouldn't be nearly as good.*

Nonetheless, in the absence of solid professional learning support, teacher concern for these students and appreciation of their challenges may have unintended and unproductive consequences for at-risk EAL students. For example, it may lead to a lowering of expectations for these students. There was some evidence of this in comments made by the teacher at School One when she said in interviews: *'I treat them* [EAL students] *the same in terms of behaviour, there's no reason why they can't give me the same behaviour ... Academically, no they can't, but I do expect them at least to have a go.'*

As low teacher expectations are known to be related to low student outcomes, the possible academic consequences of this well-intentioned attitude are significant, especially given teachers' obvious and sincere concern for their EAL students.

Overall, the teachers' comments paint a picture of dedicated educators, in the absence of strong systemic support, striving to provide education and pastoral care for this at-risk group of students. Within this educational context, we will next examine what specific pedagogical practices were employed by the teachers, and what the implications were for their students' educational progress.

Analysing lessons and looking at pedagogies

The study involved observations of lessons across all curricular areas for one school term. It required an instrument that could record pedagogies which enacted Freeman and Freeman's (2007) four principles, and thus would identify the nature of the support available to at-risk EAL students in these classrooms. These principles are consistent with Australian pedagogical frameworks such as the New South Wales Quality Teaching Framework (QTF, NSW DET, 2003). The QTF was chosen for use in the study because it provides clear descriptions of the classroom application of pedagogies aligned with Freeman and Freeman's principles. Aspects of the three Dimensions of the QTF – Intellectual Quality, Quality learning environment and Significance – guided the observations of the pedagogical practices. Definitions of each of the three Dimensions are shown in Table 4.1.

Table 4.1: Dimensions of the Quality Teaching Framework

QTF Dimension	Definition
Intellectual Quality	'pedagogy focused on producing deep understanding of important, substantive concepts, skills and ideas. Such pedagogy treats knowledge as something that requires active construction and requires students to engage in higher order thinking and to communicate substantively about what they are learning' (NSW DET, 2006, p. 10).
Quality Learning Environment	'pedagogy that creates classrooms where students and teachers work productively in an environment clearly focused on learning. Such pedagogy sets high and explicit expectations and develops positive relationships between teachers and students and among students' (NSW DET, 2006, p. 10).
Significance	'pedagogy that helps make learning more meaningful and important to students. Such pedagogy draws clear connections with students' prior knowledge and identities, with contexts outside of the classroom, and with multiple ways of knowing or cultural perspectives' (NSW DET, 2006, p. 10).

Pedagogical practices observed were recorded in extensive descriptive field notes each day for one school term.

Major findings

Analysis and synthesis of the data revealed areas of strength in current pedagogical practices, as well as some limitations.

Strengths in current practices: Social support and inclusion

Both case study classrooms were strong in provision of social support and inclusion of EAL students (aspects of Quality Learning Environments and Significance). Notable in both classrooms were teachers' practices of deliberately creating opportunities for EAL students to be socially supported through receiving their classmates' acknowledgement for their expertise and efforts. For example, when one of the EAL students at School One provided the answer to a mathematics problem in front of the class, the teacher responded: *Good girl! That shows you can take your knowledge and apply it. Well done!* On another occasion, when referring to work completed by an EAL student, she said: *Look at* [name's] *work! Excellent!* The teacher at School Two also encouraged and publically positioned one of her EAL students as competent when she said to him during an explanation in a Science class: *You need to listen, because you can do this!*

In a similar vein, another strength observed in practice was the inclusion of EAL students in all curricular activities. They were encouraged to participate, although mainly at the level of providing short responses to teachers' questions. For example, after asking the class the name of an object, the teacher at School Two encouraged one EAL student's participation saying: [Name]? *Want to have a go? Starts with g*. In general terms their inclusion was on an equal basis with that of other students.

Areas in need of development

Alongside these important strengths in practice, there were a number of areas where teaching practices could have been further strengthened. That is, there were areas where current practices did not align with what is known about evidence-based best pedagogical practice with EAL students.

Pedagogies for teaching language

As indicated, teachers were very conscious of the priority of language and literacy development for these students, and they made systematic attempts to address this. As with many mainstream teachers, they tended to focus on vocabulary development.

While vocabulary development is essential for at-risk EAL students, support for students' language development needs also to address other aspects of language and literacy – text and paragraph organisation, cohesion, sentence grammar, pronunciation and spelling. There was little evidence in the observed lessons of systematic teaching of language and literacy across those levels of language. Teachers did include some focus on metalangauge, or language for talking about language, in their classroom interaction, although this tended to focus on naming and/or revision of terms, such as in the following example: *We can have a word that's the opposite of something and that's the antonym of it. We can have something that's the same or similar, synonym same or similar, means the same thing and homonym means the same ...*

While there is considerable value in such talk about language, it tended to occur in isolation from engagement with authentic texts, and in classroom activities where there were generally limited opportunities for student participation. The focus on vocabulary and on metalanguage as terminology was consistent with teachers' recognition of students' need for language development. However, because metalanguage use was not embedded in texts from different curriculum areas, its effectiveness for EAL students was limited. So in this sense, the study showed there was a gap between teachers' awareness of students' needs, and their actual language teaching practices.

Practices that demonstrate high expectations and support high achievement

Teachers' (low) expectation of their at-risk EAL students' academic abilities appeared to be reflected in the nature of classroom activities. Field notes reveal that the bulk of the content of observed lessons was not intellectually challenging for most students and did not push them to engage with deep learning. Many of the observed class activities revolved around filling in commercially prepared 'worksheets' with only limited follow-up discussion and interpretation of content.

Feedback to EAL students regarding the quality of work that they were required to complete, and how they could improve on their current performance, tended to be very general. This was usually provided to students as part of whole-class feedback after task completion. The following example typifies the general nature of statements made about work quality. The teacher from School Two said while giving back marked books: *I've got some people who have done an excellent job on their English book. I've got other people who aren't even close to an excellent job. ... So if I thought your work was very good I've put a sticker on it* and [I] *was impressed with the sentence answers today... Pretty good ... Most people remembered a new line. Makes it look neater, doesn't it?*

While on occasion, teachers did attempt to provide further guidelines for their EAL students, these were still typically quite general and lacked the kind of intensive and explicit teaching and scaffolding of the skills needed by students for successful task completion. The following example illustrates this.

Classroom interaction related to required quality of work

[The exchange between Teacher and Student when looking at a book report stencil which students were asked to complete in response to shared book reading]

T= Teacher S= Students

T. *'What I thought'* [section on stencil] *is where you write a sentence about what you thought about that book. Do you think I'm going to like a sentence that says 'It was good'?*

Ss. *No*

T. *I would think that was good if it came from kindergarten, but in Year Three I would expect to see 'It was good because' and tell me why you thought it was good. Do you have to like it? Does it have to be a good book?*

Ss. *Nah*

T. *No, you might have thought 'I didn't really like that book because …' OK? It says* [referring to stencil], *it says 'What I thought' not what Ms* [name] *thought. It's not saying what anyone else thought, it's saying what you think. So, that's what you put down, what you think. If you thought it was a really good book because it was funny, then you write that down. And if you thought that you didn't really like it all that much, then you write 'I didn't really like this one very much' but you say why.*

For EAL students, more explicit modelling of what counted as a 'good' sentence about a book would have been useful here, as well as more explicit teaching of the kind of vocabulary and grammatical structures required to construct 'good' sentences. Students could also have been supported in the joint construction of new sentences before being asked to write independently.

Extended oral participation and higher order thinking

Analysis of lessons indicated that students had few opportunities for extended oral participation in lessons and, as a result, few opportunities to engage in substantive communication. In the observed classrooms, the majority of lessons were taught on a whole-class basis with very few instances of strategic use of group or pair work. The Initiation-Response-Evaluation (IRE) communication pattern (Sinclair & Coulthard, 1975) was dominant in all lessons and in all curriculum areas. According to

Christie (2002) instances of IRE use must be considered in the context of 'the total patterns of talk in which [it] occurs' (p. 5). Nonetheless, she also describes the pattern as 'problematic if it is allowed to prevail' (Christie, 2005, p. 40). With the dominance of the IRE pattern in the observed classrooms, there were very few opportunities for students (either from English-speaking or EAL backgrounds) to discuss and extend lesson content, or to build their spoken academic English. The reasons for the prevalence of this type of pedagogy are suggested in the following comment from the teacher at School One: *I find here* [her school], *you end up having to spoon feed them a lot and therefore you're not developing those high thinking skills, logical thinking skills as well as you would like to, but until they can do the basic skills …*

Such comments suggest that teachers were trying to meet EAL students' need for proficiency in 'basics' and language development in ways that may have unintentionally limited students' opportunities to extend their language use to 'academic talk' and also limited students' opportunities to develop higher order thinking skills.

Linking learning with students' existing knowledge

Limited opportunities for extended oral participation also meant that there were few opportunities for bringing EAL students' cultural (including L1) knowledge into the classroom to support their knowledge construction and academic English proficiency development. Although unintentional, at times this led to missed opportunities or misunderstandings between teacher and students. The following exchange between an at-risk EAL student and his teacher occurred during a lesson in which students were given a demographic survey to take home for their families to complete. The EAL student is looking at the 'Date of birth' section of the survey.

Student: *What if they* [the interviewee] *don't know when they're born?*

Teacher: *They'll know when they were born. They'll be able to fill that in for you.*

As Cranitch in Chapter 2 of this book points out, apparently simple questions, such as date of birth, can be far from straightforward for refugee students. Although each instance of the kind of misunderstanding reflected in the example is small, the accumulation of such instances contributes to the unconscious marginalisation of EAL students. This marginalisation impacts on two levels: firstly, (in this instance) it means that difficulties which some EAL students' and their families have in relation to documentation and evidencing of identity and age may not be appreciated; secondly, it denies the mainstream students in the class the opportunity for learning about alternative knowledge systems and experiences from their EAL peers.

Strengths in practice and areas for development in context

The above discussion highlights patterns of strengths and limitations in the two case study schools. Strengths were evident in the provision of social support and inclusion of EAL students. Areas needing development were related to pedagogical practices that support students to engage in high-challenge work and higher order thinking. The study suggests that strengths in current practices with EAL students can be broadly described as 'pastoral', and those areas needing development as more 'pedagogical' in nature.

The fact that strengths were in more broadly 'pastoral' practices reflects the good will teachers had for their EAL students, their willingness to support them, and their desire to see them integrated into their classes. The socially supportive and inclusive practices in which at-risk EAL students engaged met some important psychosocial needs. Indeed, the practices went some way toward enacting Freeman and Freeman's (2007) fourth principle of creating students who are confident, who value school, and who see themselves as learners. These practices developed an important psychological and physical space in which students formed valuable interpersonal relationships that could foster the risk-taking that deep learning and academic success require. In this sense, these pastoral practices were positive.

However, consistent with Foucault's (1983) contentions that pastoral care can limit the 'fields of action' available to its recipients, the finding that observed practices with EAL students were primarily 'pastoral', rather than pedagogical, had significant consequences for the learning of these students. For example, the fact that the EAL students were not routinely engaging in 'academic talk' about curriculum content and language meant that there were restricted opportunities for teachers to strongly scaffold their movement from oral language towards the academic English registers necessary for school success. For students in Year 3 this is significant – Cummins (2001) contends that from Year 4, the content and language of the curriculum become increasingly complex, specialised and de-contextualised. Without substantial, targeted support, the curriculum may become increasingly inaccessible to EAL students (even those with good oral English fluency, such as the children in this study).

Implications for school systems

Despite the very different sociocultural environments of Schools One and Two, practices with at-risk EAL students in both schools were strikingly similar. This finding suggests that such practices may occur in other non-metropolitan schools when teachers do not have access to adequate professional support in their work with these students.

As indicated, the responses to EAL students observed in this study were principally 'pastoral' in manner. This finding is consistent with the teachers' statements that they lacked confidence in their ability to meet their EAL students' learning needs. It is also consistent with teachers' comments that having these students in their classes had not led to substantial changes in the way they taught.

Outcomes from the study highlight the complex demands of teaching at-risk EAL students in the mainstream. They also highlight the need for mainstream teachers of EAL students to have access to ongoing professional learning support, especially for teachers in areas that have historically had low enrolments of these students. Ideally, such learning should provide teachers with the knowledge and skills that meet Freeman and Freeman's four principles, discussed earlier, of what constitutes effective programs for EAL students. The following section suggests content for professional learning that would build on teachers' existing strengths in practice.

Provision of professional learning to support teachers

The findings of this study indicate that teachers' supportive and inclusive practices go a considerable way to meeting Freeman and Freeman's fourth principle of fostering students who are confident, who value school and who value themselves as learners. However, findings also indicate that it may be beneficial for teachers to be offered professional learning based on Freeman and Freeman's first three principles:

1 Engage students in challenging and theme-based curriculum to foster the development of academic concepts.

2 Draw on students' cultural, linguistic and background experiences.

3 Organise collaborative activities and scaffolding instruction.

Learning for principles 1 and 2

As indicated earlier, in interviews, the case study teachers identified EAL students' language learning needs as a key priority, but said they did not have the knowledge of language required to respond pedagogically to those needs. Professional support programs for teachers, such as those in the case study schools, would benefit from explicit learning about language as a system. The approach to language underlying the new *Australian Curriculum: English* (ACARA, 2013) provides one paradigm within which to formulate the language knowledge component of professional learning for working with EAL students. In addition, knowledge of key Second Language Acquisition

(SLA) theories would support teachers' learning about language. These theories could include; the Basic Interpersonal Communicative Skills/Cognitive Academic Language Proficiency (BICS/CALP) distinction (Cummins, 1981) that explains the differences between conversational social language and the academic language required for school; Comprehensible Output theory; and the Linguistic Interdependence theory (Cummins, 1981). Strong knowledge of language and SLA would support teachers to develop appropriately challenging content and activities to foster EAL students' conceptual and language proficiency development. It would also help them to 'understand what [EAL] students bring into the classroom' (Gonzalez & Darling Hammond, 2000, p. 7), and thus facilitate their use of students' cultural, linguistic and background experiences within challenging learning activities.

Learning for principle 3

Based on the study's findings, learning to develop collaborative activities and to scaffold instruction could be organised around substantive communication, or extended oral participation and use of metalanguage. This could focus on modelling of the repertoire of evidence-based pedagogies that can be employed to promote substantive communication. Macro and micro level scaffolding (Walqui, 2006) to foster meaningful, extended oral participation by EAL students and strategies for explicit, in-context instruction about language could be modelled and subsequently practised. From these professional learning experiences, teachers might gain expertise and confidence to incorporate the necessary teaching of the language to facilitate students' engagement in higher order thinking activities. As well as developing pedagogical knowledge, teachers also need sound knowledge of the resources available to support them in making changes in practice in order to work more effectively with EAL students, for example, the 'English as an Additional Language or Dialect (EAL/D) Teacher Resource' (ACARA, 2013) accompanying the *Australian Curriculum: English*. In addition, knowledge of *The* NSW Quality Teaching Framework (NSW DET, 2003, 2006) or similar state-based frameworks like Queensland's Productive Pedagogies (Education Queensland, 2002) which provide descriptions of pedagogies proven to be productive with all learners, would also be very helpful in supporting transitions to new pedagogical practices (Coleman, 2012) with at-risk EAL learners

Conclusion

Teaching at-risk EAL students in a non-metropolitan area with low EAL enrolment presents significant pedagogical challenges to most mainstream primary teachers. The strengths in practice observed in this study came from teachers' care for their students.

However, where teachers' practices are principally restricted to the pastoral, realisation of the potential for academic achievement can be unintentionally, but seriously impeded. This study was small and as a result its findings cannot necessarily be generalised. However, it provides insights into practices in primary classes in non-metropolitan schools, and into the impact of these on EAL students. It also offers some suggestions as to how pedagogy may be strengthened through systemic provision of professional learning. It is hoped that the study, and these suggestions, may be useful to other primary teachers of at-risk EAL students who may want to develop new 'fields of action' for themselves and their students.

5

Teaching and learning practices with at-risk EAL students

Jennifer Hammond

A key theme of this book is the nature of teaching and learning practices that best support at-risk EAL students in mainstream classes. As pointed out in Chapter 1, the social and welfare needs of at-risk students have rightly received attention (Earnest, Housen & Gillieatt, 2007; Vickers, 2007; Matthews, 2008), but there has been less emphasis on teaching and learning practices that engage and support such students so that they are able to participate equitably in mainstream schooling. While there is broad agreement in society that educational achievement is a major prerequisite for access to choice in post-school study and career, in the case of at-risk students, there has often been insufficient understanding within educational systems and schools of the students' specific pedagogical needs, and of the subsequent challenges faced by teachers who are working with these students within the context of mainstream classes.

This chapter discusses the outcomes from a recently completed research project that provides some insights into the strengths and gaps in current teaching and learning practices in mainstream classes in relation to at-risk EAL students. The focus of the project was on the educational experiences of refugee and other EAL students, both before and after their transition from Intensive English Centres (IECs) to high school. Although the research was located in high schools, findings from the project have broader implications for those concerned with the educational progress of at-risk EAL students, and address more generally the nature of teaching and learning practices that are likely to support students' educational progress. The research findings presented in this chapter are therefore likely to be relevant to both primary and high school teachers who are working with at-risk students in mainstream classes.

The nature of the research project

The research consisted of a small-scale study in two Intensive English Centres (IECs) and two high schools. It concentrated on teaching and learning practices in the latter stages of enrolment in IECs and early stages of enrolment in high schools, and on the experiences of students aged between 14 and 16 years who were typically making the transition between IEC and high school in Years 8 or 9. The schools that were invited to participate in the research already had substantial programs in place to support refugee students. Our aim in the research was to build on positive models provided by these schools, but also to look closely at teaching and learning practices across a number of key curriculum subjects.

Data collection in the project included focus group interviews with school executives, teachers and students, as well as observations and recordings of lessons in core curriculum subjects. Table 5.1 summarises the range of data collected for the project.

Table 5.1: Data collected in the research

	Interviews	Lessons
IECs	15 student interviews 14 teacher interviews (including executive and subject/class teachers)	14 recorded lessons (English, Maths, History)
High schools	9 student interviews 22 teacher interviews (including executives and subject teachers)	18 recorded lessons (English, Maths, Science, Geography)

A challenge in the research was to undertake analysis of the 32 lessons in ways that enabled us to work systematically with the data generated from them, while also working at sufficient depth to gain insights into the nature of teaching and learning practices that were typical of IECs and of high schools. In developing our approach to analysis, we drew on outcomes from our previous research (Hammond and Gibbons, 2005; Michell & Sharpe, 2005; Hammond, 2008; Gibbons, 2008) that had highlighted the significance for EAL students of:

- systematic and explicit teaching of academic language and literacy embedded in across-the-curriculum programs
- targeted and differential levels of scaffolding to ensure EAL students were supported to engage in learning of curriculum concepts
- deliberate discussion of purposes for learning, at the level of Unit, Lesson and Task, so that students, including those from cultures where educational practices differed from those typical of Australian schools, were helped to understand the purposes and directions of learning.

We also drew on the NSW Quality Teaching Framework (DET, NSW, 2003; 2004). The resulting combination of features reflected our assumptions that successful programs for at-risk students must involve both high-challenge and high-support programs. Table 5.2 summarises the combined features addressed in our system of analysis:

Table 5.2: Elements and aspects of pedagogy used in analysis of lessons

	Intellectual Quality	Quality Learning Environment	Significance
Elements from Quality Teaching Framework	Deep knowledge Deep understanding Substantive communication	Engagement High expectations Social support	Background knowledge Cultural knowledge Connectedness Inclusivity
Pedagogical features from previous research	Academic language focus	Explicit goals Scaffolding	

(See Hammond, 2014a for further details of the project as a whole and of the approach and procedures used in analysis of lessons).

Findings from the research

The strength of research schools in supporting at-risk EAL students

While the major focus in this Chapter, and of the book as a whole, is on teaching and learning practices, it is impossible to discuss educational practices for at-risk EAL students without first recognising the significance of students' welfare and wellbeing. A positive, safe and supportive learning environment is essential for any student, but it is an especially important prerequisite for effective learning for at-risk EAL students (see Chapter 1). As others have argued (Munns, Sawyer & Cole, 2013), social and emotional dimensions of classrooms do impact on students' learning. Findings regarding the nature of learning environments in our research schools were therefore significant.

The research found that participating schools were particularly strong in the following areas:

- providing welcoming and supportive learning environments at whole-school levels and within individual classrooms

- providing a range of innovative and creative programs at whole-school level and within classrooms that specifically targeted students' emotional and educational needs, and supported them in their transition from IEC to high school.

As indicated earlier, schools were invited to participate in the research because they already had programs in place that were designed to support their refugee and other EAL students. Thus on one level, it was not surprising that all sources of data confirmed welfare support was a particular strength of the schools. However, the extent of that support, and the range of innovative, strong and effective programs that were in place were considerably greater than we had expected.

The programs in place within schools acknowledged students' strengths and supported them at a variety of levels. These programs included:

- **supporting students in early stages of enrolment at school:**
  - availability of bilingual support staff to help with enrolment and to mediate between students, school and community
  - availability of school counsellors to support students as necessary (especially important for students who had experienced prior and/or ongoing trauma)
  - orientation programs when students first arrived in school that made students feel welcome and taught them about the school and its culture; the programs supported the students during their first weeks at school and provided opportunities for them to voice any concerns
- **supporting students' ongoing welfare:**
  - providing a Learning and Support Team in the school with responsibility for students' welfare and wellbeing – the team provided a point of personal contact that was especially important in the initial phase of enrolment at school
  - strategies to find some financial support to address emergencies experienced by students and their families
  - availability of staff who were willing to support individual students as and where this was needed
- **supporting students in their academic study:**
  - availability of EAL teachers on staff and extra time for these teachers to work with specific groups of students in response to needs as they arose
  - parallel English programs that specifically supported students' ongoing language development, while also engaging with study of English texts
  - Refugee Transition Programs providing additional language and literacy support for refugee students, with a program coordinator aiming to provide refugee students with access to high-challenge academic work while also developing the language, literacy and study skills necessary to enable them to engage with this high-challenge work

- volunteers who worked with individual students during class, especially to support students' literacy development
- after school homework program (with support from university student volunteers).

The high schools also included a range of programs that encouraged students to think forward to their future life beyond schools. They provided links with community and educational organisations such as TAFE and local universities outside of school; and they built on positive role models from successful ex-students who were invited back to school to talk to students. Although some programs were specific to high schools, the kinds of programs, and the overall range of support that they provided within the research schools, provide models that are equally relevant to primary and high schools.

Significantly, in all the research schools, supportive and positive learning environments were evident at a whole-school level as well as in individual lessons. While executive staff members were pivotal in establishing and supporting many of the programs that operated at a whole-school level, teachers and bilingual support staff contributed to the programs and more generally to the safe, mutually respectful, and supportive nature of the learning environment in the school. Interviews with both teachers and students provided evidence of the extent of additional support provided by individual teachers in their own time: in extra homework support; in ensuring students had access to financial support for uniforms and excursions where necessary; and in assisting with travel to and from excursions as necessary. Lesson observations also confirmed that teachers interacted in respectful and equitable ways with students, and they brought a level of humour and fun to their lessons. In their interviews, students reported feeling safe and supported at school. They recognised that teachers were sympathetic and genuinely 'there' for them and they appreciated this.

An important contributing factor to the positive school environment was the strength and resilience of the students themselves. Despite the substantial challenges that refugee and other at-risk EAL students had faced in adapting to life and schooling in Australia, those we encountered in the research project overwhelmingly showed a positive attitude to their lives and to their futures in Australia. In their interviews, students stated they were determined to do something substantial with their lives, and they were perceptive about what this might entail. They also revealed very positive attitudes to school. As one student explained: *school is preparing us for life … it's preparing us for our future, and giving us more inspiration for other things.*

The findings in regard to school learning environments and students' wellbeing and welfare are significant. They show that the schools provided the essential basis for students' educational success – the basis from which a more detailed focus on teaching and learning for both teachers and of students becomes possible.

Current pedagogical practices: The balance of challenge and support

While a positive learning environment provides the necessary basis for effective learning, it is not enough. As argued in chapter 1, equitable access for all students, including at-risk EAL student involves access to high-challenge, high-support programs (Hammond, 2014b).

Research outcomes showed there was some inconsistency in schools in the extent to which students were provided with high-challenge, high-support programs. While quite a number of lessons presented students with sustained and consistent access to challenging ideas and concepts, lessons overall were weaker when it came to ensuring students were able to understand and engage with those ideas and concepts. There was little evidence of students being able to provide information, arguments and reasoning, or of asking and exploring genuine questions in a sustained way, or of engaging in deep discussion about key curriculum concepts. This meant that although quite a number of students had access to high-challenge curriculum content, they did not always have access to the levels of support that would enable them to understand and engage at a deep level with that curriculum content.

In their interviews, teachers participating in the research spoke of conflicting pressures to 'get through' mandatory curriculum content while also trying to ensure all students were able to understand and engage deeply with that work. They reported that this pressure was increased when they worked with at-risk EAL students who had experienced minimal or disrupted schooling prior to coming to Australia. They spoke of their uncertainty about the best ways of meeting the educational needs of these students who generally had low levels of literacy in both their mother tongue and in English, and who had substantial gaps in their knowledge of educational concepts. Teachers commented on the considerable pressure they faced in trying to juggle the needs of students who were at very different educational levels and who had very diverse emotional and educational needs.

This overall pattern of findings is consistent with outcomes from research undertaken by Miller and her colleagues (Miller, 2009; Miller & Windle, 2010; Windle & Miller, 2012). In this research, high school teachers, in particular, reported pressure to get through the curriculum, and a lack of time and resources, which resulted in them being unable to support their at-risk EAL students, especially those who had low levels of literacy, in ways that they would like. Similar challenges have been acknowledged by other researchers (Dooley, 2009; Brown, Miller & Mitchell, 2006; Cranitch, 2010).

Strengthening teaching and learning practices

The conflicting pressures identified by teachers of getting through the curriculum, while also taking the time to ensure all students understand and engage deeply with key curriculum concepts, are very real. The resulting dilemma is one faced by all teachers. While there is no simple solution to this dilemma, outcomes from the research offer insights into some of the ways in which these conflicting pressures can be reduced. Specifically, outcomes suggest ways in which teaching and learning practices in mainstream classes could be refined to better support at-risk EAL students. The research findings suggest the need for more:

- emphasis on scaffolding and 'message abundancy'
- systematic and explicit teaching of language and literacy across the curriculum
- consistent and explicit discussion of purposes and significance of learning
- emphasis on 'unpacking' of assessment tasks.

Scaffolding and 'message abundancy'

The kind of targeted and differential pedagogical support that is available to refugee and other at-risk EAL students is crucial to their educational success. From interviews, it was evident that teachers were clearly aware of this, and they highlighted the importance of specific strategies that contributed to this support. Although teachers did not necessarily use the term themselves, their discussions pointed to the significance of the metaphor of 'scaffolding'. This term refers to specific kinds of support that pushes students to work just beyond their current capabilities (Maybin, Mercer & Steirer, 1992; Hammond & Gibbons, 2005). It also refers to pre-planned and point-of-need support that explicitly and consistently recognises and addresses students' language and curriculum learning needs. This is typically done through planning, selection and sequencing of whole-class, group and individual tasks to enable differential levels of support and to provide opportunities for handover as students become more capable and independent as learners. As indicated earlier, our previous research had highlighted the significance of scaffolding in ensuring EAL students were supported in their engagement with key educational concepts.

Although teachers in our research schools were aware of the importance of high levels of support for students, analysis of lessons pointed to some discrepancy between teachers' awareness, and the extent to which that awareness was translated into systematic and targeted support in at least some classrooms. This finding is especially important for refugee and other at-risk EAL students, and explains why some students were not able to engage with challenging curriculum content.

In interviews, students as well as teachers were articulate about the strategies that 'helped' refugee and other at-risk EAL students, and responses from the two groups in many ways mirrored each other. While neither group actually used the term 'message abundancy', this notion arose again and again. The term, introduced by Gibbons (2003; 2009b), refers to ways in which students can be provided with access again and again (abundantly) to similar messages or concepts, via different modes of meaning (semiotic modes). Access to message abundancy ensures that students who may not understand a concept the first time it is introduced, can visit and revisit the same concept via a range of activities and a range of modes. These may include a variety of hands-on activities, visual support, group discussion, working with multimodal texts, reading tasks, and written charts. Thus message abundancy is a component of scaffolding. For refugee and other at-risk EAL students, access to message abundancy is especially important as it enables them to engage with educational concepts while having time to visit and revisit the English language that is necessary for their developing understanding of those concepts, and for their abilities to talk, read and write about such concepts.

When discussing how they helped their students, teachers captured the notion of 'message abundancy' by describing strategies that enabled students to visit and revisit similar concepts. They referred to the need for:

- demonstrating as well as explaining
- modelling, modelling, and modelling again
- planning learning activities that involved small steps
- providing multiple opportunities for repetition and practice
- providing carefully structured support within activities
- very gradual handover
- building in success
- using Information Technology to provide additional opportunities to revisit specific concepts (both in class and for homework)
- working between concrete and more general/ abstract concepts
- never assuming students had prior cultural/Australian/school knowledge.

An example of a task that incorporates some of these features (small steps; opportunities for revision and practice; gradual handover; use of IT) was described by one of the teachers. The task consisted of a dictation activity where one student must read a text, then dictate what they can remember from the text to another student who writes the remembered text onto a laptop. In the process of reconstructing the text, the students negotiate sentence sequences, grammatical structure, spelling and punctuation. The resulting text is then read to larger groups of students, and further negotiation of remembered details and of language features takes place. Students then email the completed version to others. The task thus involves listening, speaking, reading and writing, as well as on-line editing. It also involves discussion of language features and requires students to justify specific choices that they make in the reconstruction of the text. Teachers reported using such tasks strategically in response to students' specific abilities and needs – in this case either as revision of familiar work or as a way of introducing students to new texts or sections of texts.

When discussing what teachers do that most helps them, students identified strategies that were similar to those identified by teachers. These included:

- clear teacher explanations (and re-explanations as necessary) – one student explained: *Our teacher asks us if we don't understand anything or we don't understand any words and then she explains it to us or she writes it on the board and then she explains us until we understand.*
- hands-on activities in class (such as science experiments); physical demonstrations and visual support; students said that the process of experiencing something and seeing it before being required to talk and write about it was helpful;
- opportunities for observations and experiences through incursions and excursions where students see *real things*
- support in learning vocabulary – One student explained how her teacher helped: *She say, you know what 'room' is? 'Room' is like this, and she write and she draw and stuff like this. So she explains without even asking her.*

- online tasks that address similar concepts to those discussed in class – students found using laptops was both fun and useful; they particularly liked being able to work online and do homework online
- group discussions – despite describing themselves as being too shy to talk in front of their class, many students said they liked opportunities to talk through ideas and information: '*cause we can share ideas; like everybody brings their own idea and then bring it together to make it strong. Not just one person.*
- prior reading – students identified reading as a major challenge, but when teachers introduced a text by reading to students and explaining words, they said it helped them get the general sense and meaning of the text prior to reading it themselves: *If there's like a paragraph, like very important that we really need to understand ... our teachers, they read that for us because they know that if one of us reads it the other ones might not understand.*
  After this students could work independently and look more closely at specific meaning of words.
- opportunities to ask for help where necessary – students consistently highlighted the value of clear teacher explanations, and of teachers' willingness to explain work again when they asked for help.

The overall challenge here lies in ensuring that such strategies are systematically included in lessons and are linked with explicit teaching of language and literacy.

> In previous research, we found that designing programs around Essential Questions (that is, key questions that provide relevant and genuine inquiry into big ideas and core curriculum content), as well a final Rich Task (that is, a task of substantial intellectual and educational challenge) was particularly helpful in ensuring programs were intellectually challenging and engaging. These 'tools' provided a frame whereby classroom tasks could be selected and sequenced so that high levels of scaffolding and 'message abundancy' were 'designed-in' to ensure students had access to systematic and targeted support. Such tools are likely to be relevant to both primary and secondary teachers who are addressing issues of challenge and support in their own educational contexts (See Gibbons, 2008; 2009b; Hammond & Gibbons, 2005; Hammond, 2014b for further details of work with Essential Questions and Rich Tasks).

Research findings in regard to scaffolding and message abundancy inevitably overlapped with those regarding teaching of academic language and literacy.

Explicit and systematic teaching of language and literacy across the curriculum

Teaching academic language and literacy is central to the educational success of refugee and other at-risk EAL students. While all school students face the task of engaging with demands of academic language and literacy as they progress through high school, these demands are considerably greater for at-risk students who cannot build on prior knowledge of oral English, and in some cases, cannot rely on prior knowledge of literacy.

From their interviews, it was evident that both teachers and students were very much aware of the importance of academic English development, and they considered it to be the students' highest priority. Teachers reported that they regarded themselves as teachers of English as well as Science, Maths, History and other subjects. Analysis of lessons however, pointed to a more complex picture, and, overall, we found there was considerable variation in the extent to which lessons systematically and explicitly incorporated and taught language across the curriculum.

Comments from teachers in their interviews were relevant to this issue. While many teachers said they were 'reasonably confident' in teaching language and literacy, most said they would like more knowledge of EAL-specific strategies, and of ways of systematically and explicitly teaching language and literacy across the curriculum. Such comments are consistent with previous research findings that show, while teachers are aware of the importance of academic language and literacy education with their students, many lack confidence in their knowledge of how to teach it in their lessons (Hammond & Macken-Horarik, 2001; Macken-Horarik, Love & Unsworth, 2011; Jones & Chen, 2012).

The importance of building knowledge about language and knowledge of language teaching is acknowledged in recent Australian educational initiatives. For example, the English component of the new Australian Curriculum (ACARA, 2012), with its three major strands of Language, Literacy and Literature, highlights the role of language in learning, and points to the importance of teachers' understanding of increasing demands of academic language and literacy. The EAL/D: Teachers' Resource (ACARA, 2011) similarly acknowledges the importance of language learning and teaching, and the National Professional Standards for Teachers (AITSL, 2011, Standard 2.5) prioritises supporting students' literacy and numeracy development. These initiatives legitimise and reinforce the need to address knowledge about language and language teaching. However, our research suggests that, especially for teachers working with at-risk EAL students, a further step is needed – opportunities to access ongoing, substantial and well-resourced professional development programs that support teachers to embed effective teaching of language and literacy across the curriculum.

Purposes and significance of learning

Our research addressed the extent to which purposes of learning were made explicit to students during lessons, and the extent to which connections were made between curriculum knowledge and the broader world beyond school. These features capture an orientation to learning that is important for all students – one that enables them to understand there is a broader purpose and significance to educational knowledge; and that schooling is about more than assessment tasks and examinations. This orientation is especially important for refugee and other at-risk EAL students who may be struggling to understand the learning purposes of specific classroom practices – practices such as hands-on activities, group work or school excursions that were not part of their schooling experiences prior to coming to Australia. Students may also be struggling to understand the relevance and connections of specific curriculum topics that may seem remote from their own prior experiences and lives.

Our analysis of lessons showed there was generally some explanation of what students would be doing in any lesson (that is, there was some explanation of what curriculum content would be covered in the lesson), and some connections were made to what students had learned in previous lessons. However, there was relatively little systematic discussion of why it was important to study particular topics or concepts; what the purposes of specific units, or lessons were; or of what students were expected to learn as they engaged in specific tasks.

A clearer emphasis on the purpose and significance of learning could be achieved by more explicit discussion of purpose of learning specific topics. This would include making unit and lessons goals more explicit (for example, *to develop students' understandings of basic elements of the earth; to investigate how knowledge of elements can be of use in the world beyond school*); it would include more discussion of expected learning outcomes from sequences of classroom activities and tasks (*This experiment will help you learn about the process of filtration* ...); and more emphasis on the significance of educational knowledge and learning in connection both with students' prior learning and experiences, and with broader world knowledge (*How do scientists classify matter? Who can think of ways that we use sieving in the kitchen?*) That is, there could be more emphasis on WHY learning about specific topics and concepts is important and relevant, and HOW it is significant to life in and out of school.

'Unpacking' of assessment tasks

The most frequent topic of concern, and the one that generated most discussion in students' interviews, was assessment tasks. Students agreed that assessment tasks and examinations were the most challenging and stressful aspect of mainstream school. Science assessment tasks in particular seemed to generate high levels of anxiety.

Part of the challenge involved students being sufficiently organised to begin assessment tasks early enough to allow sufficient time for completion, rather than putting off work until close to due dates. However, the major part of the challenge for students was to understand what was required with assessment tasks. In interviews, students indicated they had difficulties working out the nature of the curriculum content that they were expected to engage with; and they had more difficulty working out how they should approach the assignment – what text types were required and how they needed to structure those text types. Students also expressed anxiety about examinations and were concerned about the time it took them to read examination questions with the consequence that their time for responding was limited.

In interviews, a number of teachers indicated they already had strategies in place to assist students with assessment tasks. For example, many teachers provided one-on-one support for students who were concerned about assessment tasks. Some teachers encouraged students to submit drafts of assessment tasks so that they could receive and respond to feedback prior to the due date of submission. While very helpful, such strategies depended on students being sufficiently organised to be able to spend time with teachers, or to submit their assessment tasks in time to receive feedback. Other teachers had provided alternative, less demanding assessment tasks for at-risk EAL students, but in order to be fair to other students, they deducted a number of marks if students chose to do the alternative task. While students appreciated this option, they were concerned about losing marks if they chose the easier option.

Students' concerns highlight the more general need for teachers to spend time 'unpacking' assessment tasks and examination requirements. At-risk EAL students may not have had opportunities to learn organisational skills that are commonly associated with formal schooling. Thus 'unpacking' of assignment tasks is likely to include working with students on planning timetables for completion of tasks, and on details of how they should prepare in terms of prior research and reading (including strategies that show them how to undertake this prior work). In addition, 'unpacking' includes very detailed discussion of what assessment tasks require of students: What knowledge of curriculum content; and what text type. It also involves providing 'good' models, and detailed discussion (more 'unpacking') of those models to increase students' understanding of requirements of assessment tasks.

In many ways discussion of 'unpacking' assessment tasks overlaps with the previous discussion of the need for more language teaching. Students' comments point, in particular, to their uncertainty regarding the language requirements of assessment tasks. While the demands of assessment tasks are likely to continue to cause stress, by 'unpacking' the content and language requirements of these tasks, teachers can, at least to some extent, alleviate their students' anxiety. The better the students understand the requirements of assessment tasks, the more likely they are to complete the tasks successfully.

Implications from the research for teachers of at-risk EAL students

As with any small research project, findings here need to be treated with caution. They do not provide 'proof' of any kind; rather, they point to pedagogical patterns that are likely to be typical of those in schools with similar student populations. Findings from this project may therefore help others who are interested in analysis of their own educational contexts, and in refining teaching and learning practices for their at-risk EAL students. Below, the relevant implications are discussed further.

Models of support provided by the research schools

The IECs and high schools that participated in the research provided very strong models of supportive and welcoming learning environments that benefited refugee and other at-risk EAL students. These environments were evident at the level of the whole school, as well as individual classrooms, and included a range of programs that addressed welfare and educational needs of students. See earlier discussion on pages 64-65 that included a list of programs and strategies in the schools that are likely to be relevant for both primary and high schools.

Refining classroom practices to give students systematic support with intellectually challenging curricula

At-risk EAL students had access to high challenge curriculum content in a number of their lessons, but had less access to the high levels of systematic support that was necessary for them to engage intellectually with that curriculum content. This pattern is consistent with outcomes from other research (Windle & Miller, 2012), and is likely to be typical of what happens in other schools. Outcomes from the research suggest that ways of addressing this issue could include:

- more attention to scaffolding, and especially to the way in which 'message abundancy' is incorporated into selection and sequencing of classroom activities
- more systematic and explicit focus on academic language and literacy development across the curriculum
- more focus on explicit goals and expected learning outcomes: that is, more emphasis on WHY learning about specific topics and concepts is important and relevant, and HOW it is significant to life in and out of school
- more consistent systematic 'unpacking' of requirements and expectations in relation to assessment tasks and exams.

Professional programs to support teachers of at-risk EAL students

At-risk EAL students who have had minimal or disrupted schooling, and who generally have very low levels of literacy in both mother tongue and English pose the greatest challenge for teachers. Targeted professional development programs that address the kinds of pedagogical practices that teachers could incorporate into their programs would be of great benefit. Such programs would address:

- working with hands-on activities that require use of oral language-accompanying-action
- working from concrete experiences, and building gradually to more general and abstract understandings of educational concepts
- building on students' oral language to develop understandings of literacy
- building in numerous small steps in learning
- highlighting the importance of 'message abundancy' in programs
- articulating ways of planning and implementing programs that are characterised by high 'message abundancy' to address specific needs of students.

In addition, our research confirms previous findings that teachers generally lack confidence to teach academic language and literacy. It points to the importance for all teachers who work with refugee and other at-risk EAL students of having ongoing access to relevant professional support to address this issue. Such support could include:

- assisting teachers to extend their knowledge of academic language and literacy, and ways of incorporating that knowledge in different curriculum areas

- encouraging teachers to obtain relevant EAL qualifications
- implementing the *Teaching English Language Learners across the Curriculum* (TELL) professional learning program, or equivalent, across the school
- working within the framework of educational initiatives such as the national Australian Curriculum (ACARA, 2012) and EAL/D resources (ACARA, 2011); the National Professional Standards for Teachers (AITSL, 2011) to address implications for refugee and other at-risk EAL students.

Some of the program features and research findings addressed in this chapter are specific to high schools, but many are not. The research outcomes and implications for teaching and learning practices are therefore likely to be relevant to primary as well as high school teachers who are working with at-risk EAL students. Hopefully, they will be of use to all those working with at-risk students in their educational journey in Australia.

Acknowledgements

The research discussed in this chapter was funded by the NSW Department of Education and Communities (Multicultural Programs Unit, 2011). It was undertaken in collaboration with Jane Wallace, Refugee Student Programs Advisor, and with support from Christine Tiekle, Intensive English Program Advisor. I would like to thank the IEC and high school staff and students who generously enabled us to undertake the research.

6

Intensive language scaffolding across the curriculum: An EAL literacy model

Jennifer Miller & Miranda McCallum

Students with interrupted schooling and low literacy are highly at risk of failing at school, and meeting their needs remains a critical challenge for teachers. In a recent report of research from the University of Western Sydney, 'developing [students'] proficiency in English language and literacy' was in the top three priorities of 90% of 5128 teachers surveyed, and top area of need for 64% (see Watkins, et al., 2013). Gibbons (2009b, p. 4) states, 'gaps in literacy in a second language may constitute a major barrier to further engagement and success in learning'. Clearly there are social, cultural and affective factors that also impact on the learning of these students. The challenge is to be responsive to the affective and welfare needs of students while maintaining the highest possible academic expectations and cognitive challenge (see Gibbons, 2009b; Hammond, 2008). How can we be caring and supportive of these students, while being rigorous and challenging in our teaching? As teachers work to engage students in texts, genres and critical and creative tasks, many at-risk EAL students are still struggling with spelling, handwriting, decoding and everyday vocabulary. There is a need to ensure the foundational aspects of language and literacy are addressed, but in a way that both challenges and supports students, and moves them towards more complex work.

This chapter proposes a model of pedagogy that integrates literacy and second language acquisition principles, and which targets EAL students who have low levels of literacy. The model is the outcome of a longitudinal research project funded by the Australian Research Council (ARC), which investigated the 'language in content' needs of at-risk middle school EAL students who struggle with school-based literacy in a range of subject areas. Some of the study's findings are briefly summarised here.

Findings of the study

The study looked at four middle years classrooms in English, Maths and Science, and aimed to investigate literacy and content pedagogy which engages and supports at-risk learners. The four classrooms were observed for a combined 100 hours over three semesters, by means of videotaping, collecting class materials, and taking copious field notes. Teachers and students were interviewed, and reading and writing tests administered to 45 students. The tests showed that the range of literacy levels in some classrooms spanned up to six years, and that at-risk students struggled with semantic and syntactic decoding skills (Miller, Keary & Windle, 2012). The observations and interviews revealed four areas of concern which were related to:

- planning
- the balance of oral and written activity in classrooms,
- the explicit teaching of language, and
- feedback.

First, teachers reported feeling under pressure to cover the curriculum in the given period of time, which limited their planning time for differentiation. When teachers feel rushed to cover content, it is easy to skip vital scaffolding stages, consequently limiting the opportunities for students to practise applying new knowledge before moving on to new material. Students can then struggle to retain key concepts and language. From the research we concluded that the way teachers plan can go some way to address this concern (Miller, Windle, & Yazdanpanah, 2014). Additionally, providing well-scaffolded tasks that students can tackle autonomously with some success can help to reduce pressure on teachers, while providing cognitively and linguistically challenging activities for students (McCallum & Miller, 2013a).

Second, although teachers stressed that reading skills and written English were the primary needs of their students, classrooms were dominated by oral language activities and plenty of teacher talk. Oral language provides a vital link to writing, particularly when it is 'academic' or talk about thinking and ideas. Finding a bridge from talk to written practice is very important in literacy development, along with the systematic movement back and forth between the two. It is the balancing of the quality of talk, and the amount of talk which matters. Our research showed a need to limit lengthy teacher explanations and to get students on to reading and written tasks more promptly during lessons. It is tempting when students do not understand, to simply explain further, but sometimes teachers do so much of the work, students don't have to read the text at all

(Yang & Wilson, 2006). In addition, when students' speaking skills exceed their reading or writing skills, as is generally the case in language learning, teachers sometimes allow them to talk about things for much of the lesson, with insufficient explicit attention to written forms, and individual practice in these forms. Talk, especially when it is elaborated and 'literate', is vital to support writing. However, a conscious systematic move to writing and reading in most lessons, and a more balanced skill focus is required.

Third, in classes with high numbers of EAL learners with limited literacy, the importance of vocabulary development and teaching comprehension skills cannot be overestimated (Wagner, Muse & Tannenbaum, 2007). Tied to this is the related conceptual development that students need in a new subject area. Students cannot engage with complex mainstream texts if they are unfamiliar with the vocabulary and the core concepts needed for comprehension. More importantly, teachers cannot assume concepts and vocabulary have been understood or acquired, even if they have been 'covered' previously. Anyone who has endeavored to learn a new language, or indeed mastered one, understands just how hard it is, and how much work, practice and repetition is involved. When you add the complexity of a new language to the complexity of unfamiliar concepts and content in Science, Maths, or subject English, how much more challenging is it for EAL students? The focused communicative teaching of vocabulary and structures, informed by second language literacy principles can help students move towards reading and using more complex and challenging texts (Miller & Windle, 2010). Such principles include comprehensible input, language recycling, grammar activities, the teaching of comprehension skills, and a developmental sequence.

Finally, although teachers knew monitoring and feedback are important, we observed very little formative assessment in lessons. Again, this may be due to limited time, so that teachers tend to rely on informal observation in class, or levels of participation. But this way of determining student understanding is unreliable for a number of reasons. Formative assessment has been defined as 'the lived, daily embodiment of a teacher's desire to refine practice based on a keener understanding of current levels of student performance' (NCTE, 2014). Our research indicated a clear need for more formative assessment tasks as a routine aspect of teaching, to inform teachers about where to pitch their lessons, to get more detailed feedback on student progress, and for ongoing planning.

The literacy model proposed here is a response to some of these concerns we have discussed. In what follows, we provide a rationale, and a diagrammatic model for scaffolding literacy in an additional language. We then explain each of its components in more detail, with examples where relevant. We have tried to offer a practical guide to this approach for English and other content areas. The model is designed to support planning a unit, topic, or single lesson and to guide the teaching approach. The EAL terminology used in this chapter can be found in the glossary at the end of the book.

Model rationale and context

Many literacy models exist to guide teachers in assisting all students to access the curriculum and develop their language knowledge and skills (Luke & Freebody, 1999; Gibbons, 2008; Cummins, 2000), and they have informed the model presented here. However for EAL students, the 'A for additional' in the acronym is a reminder that what works for monolingual students may not be enough for second or additional language learners (Miller & Windle, 2010). Our understanding of literacy aligns with the literacy strand within the proposed Australian Curriculum, (ACARA, 2015) which incorporates:

- fluency in the sound–letter correspondences of English
- an expanding reading, writing and speaking vocabulary and a grasp of grammatical and textual patterns sufficient to understand and learn from texts encountered in and out of school, and to create effective and innovative texts.

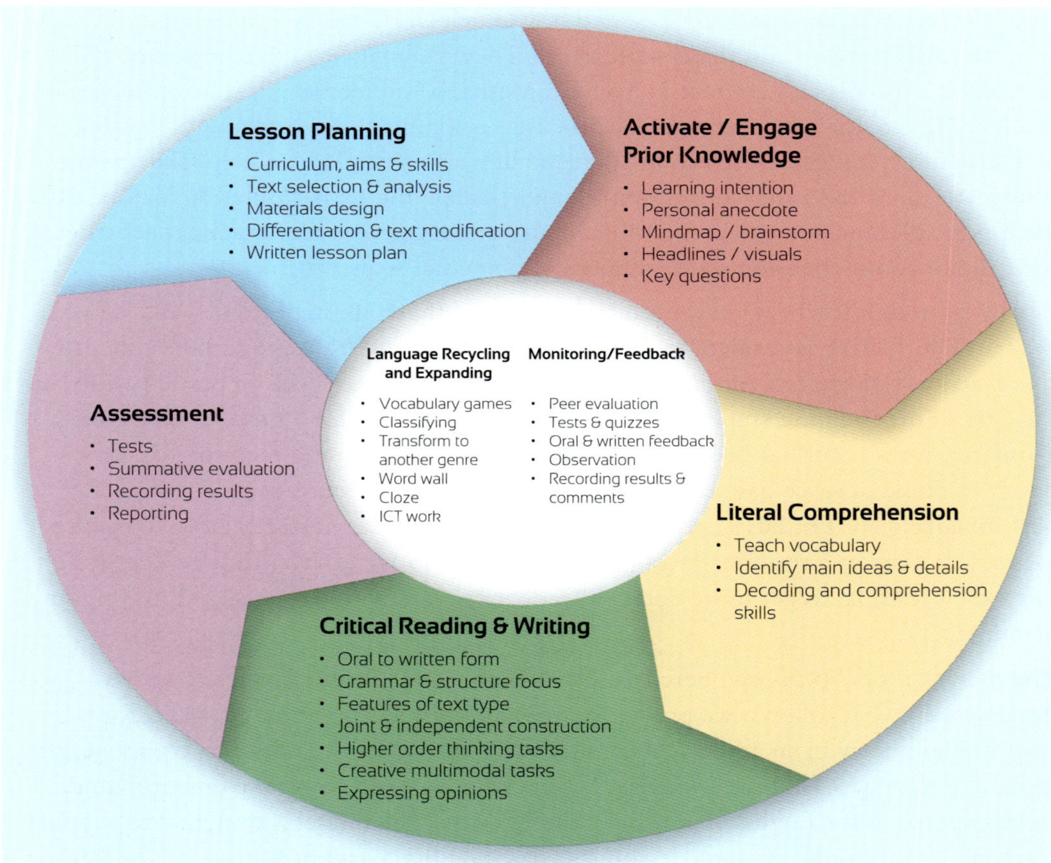

Figure 6.1: Intensive language scaffolding across the curriculum

To address the specific needs of low-literacy EAL students across the curriculum, our model (Figure 6.1), blends key principles from communicative second language and literacy pedagogies, including a detailed planning phase, extensive explicit teaching, systematic recycling and practice of language structures, a strong vocabulary and comprehension focus and consistent monitoring of progress.

The pedagogy model proposed here has a key overarching goal, namely the integration of intensive language scaffolding through all dimensions of learning and teaching. The five sections of the model represent phases in a teaching and learning cycle. The two core areas (language recycling and monitoring/feedback) are a reminder that a language focus can be embedded in all phases of a unit. Although some kind of logical, sequential movement through the phases is suggested, teachers do not need to be bound by a lock-step process. The bullet points within each phase of the model suggest possible language focuses and dimensions of literacy. They outline activities, skills, teaching strategies and student learning practices that may be appropriate at each phase. These are described more fully later in this chapter. In language and content learning, students need to recycle elements of language until concepts, structures, vocabulary and competencies become more automatic and are acquired. Such recycling is related to what Gibbons (2003) calls 'message abundancy'.

The interrelatedness of all phases will be apparent to experienced teachers, who understand that tight sequential structures do not serve the interests of all students. The phases represent dimensions of good practice and cannot exist in isolation. The model has been developed to assist mainstream teachers in meeting the needs of low-literacy EAL students, especially within classes requiring a degree of differentiation. While it targets EAL students, the approach and teaching strategies suggested would also assist other students struggling with language and/or literacy in a mainstream school setting. We have often been told this is the kind of explicit scaffolded approach that works for all students who do not have age-appropriate literacy levels.

Teachers may not always think of themselves as 'content teachers,' but it is difficult to imagine any lesson that is 'content free.' In primary English teaching and learning for example, the content may include imaginative texts, informational texts, persuasive texts, topics about the students themselves and the world, issues, genre features, grammar, the nature of learning itself and many other things. While the model provides a diagrammatic tool for teachers, we now look at each phase of it in more detail, including description, links and examples where relevant. Examples used in the following sections are drawn from a sample unit on ecosystems for at-risk middle school EAL learners. The unit provides support for students encountering challenging mainstream content. The unit reflects key aspects of the model, and shows how to integrate language and content. Teachers can access the full unit and guidelines online (see McCallum & Miller, 2013b).

Planning phase

Knowledge of the educational, cultural and social backgrounds of students is paramount to successful planning (Burgoyne & Hull, 2007; Cassity & Gow, 2006). Gibbons (2009b) stresses that students' prior linguistic knowledge needs to be the starting point in planning learning objectives. For low-literacy EAL students in particular, this is vital. As an integral part of planning, systematic monitoring and feedback are necessary to ensure that lessons are pitched at the right level so that key skills and content can be learned. Before commencing a new unit, key content and language objectives within the unit need to be identified, and integrated into tasks. These suggestions may help:

- start from curriculum guidelines
- ensure texts and tasks are cognitively challenging
- choose texts that are accessible and relevant to the learners and modify if necessary
- analyse the texts to identify (and list) vocabulary, text features and structures that may be challenging for students
- include tasks across all macro skills (reading, writing, speaking and listening)
- think about how to maximise interaction and recycling of structures
- attend to differentiation for a range of students
- develop or adapt activities, tasks and worksheets.

Most mainstream texts written for students with chronological age-appropriate schooling are not comprehensible to struggling EAL learners. If teachers use the same text for all students, this often results in heavily teacher-centred scaffolding for EAL students who need help. Such classrooms may have high levels of teacher talk, or sometimes simple handouts that require no talk at all. If some students cannot read the text, our approach is rather to modify it, and to provide support for students to learn in a more autonomous and active way. The priority is to find texts and activities that are both challenging and achievable. Text modification is an interim measure to get students working. Once they are confident with accessible texts, they can progress to more difficult materials, which is also the principle of graded readers. This also makes sense given the wide range of reading ages often present within a single classroom. As part of planning therefore, teachers should try to plan multiple entry points for students who will work at different rates. Resources that enable student autonomy are therefore essential. To allow students to negotiate content at their own pace, initial content must be delivered using written and visual material and brief, simple explanations. The selection of texts should also take into account the vocabulary students already possess. Modifying texts is part of the planning process and involves reducing the density of new words and unnecessarily complex sentence structures. Strategies for doing this are outlined at the end of this section. Planning also has a vital role in ensuring a balance between oral and written activities.

Identifying the key language that students need to effectively negotiate key concepts in a new topic is a vital element of the planning process (Gibbons, 2009b). Unit plans should specify key concepts, vocabulary, language structures, as well as integrate texts with a balance of oral and written activities. This will ensure that knowledge and skills are built up in a strategic interconnected sequence. Careful planning also avoids the practice of doing activities based on the resources that are at hand rather than the resources needed to enable effective learning (Miller, Windle and Yazdanpanah, 2014).

In summary, planning is a complex and vital part of effective pedagogy, although teachers are increasingly beset by multiple tasks that detract from the time needed to plan effectively. Finding ways to streamline planning and share resources remains an ongoing challenge for all teachers. In the framework of the model, the planning phase must be seen as the baseline preparation for all other phases of teaching and learning. Text modification, even though temporary, is part of planning. It is important to strike a balance between retaining key information or arguments, and simplifying the text to make it more accessible. We suggest several strategies to do this:

- choose texts that mirror mainstream materials provided to other students in the class, so EAL students see it a 'real work' (not 'busy work')
- simplify and reduce the number of new content words
- break complex sentence into simpler forms
- reduce the use of passive voice
- limit complex noun forms initially
- avoid too many culturally specific terms and idiomatic language
- allow for more redundancy or repetition than the original
- add visual support
- keep it short (around 200 words) to enable students to understand and practise key concepts and vocabulary.

Activate and engage prior knowledge phase

Teachers in our study were aware of the importance of building on students' prior knowledge when introducing new material, and were aware their students did not share the same knowledge as mainstream students. Students may be language learners but they come to class with diverse life experiences that may be valuable resources for learning. Teachers can help students to make connections between the world within and beyond the classroom (Burgoyne & Hull, 2007). Certain topics lend themselves to such connections more easily than others.

We suggest including strategies to activate prior learning such as eliciting students' personal anecdotes or modelling key concepts through hands-on activities. Extensive use of visuals, real life props, and multimedia are essential in triggering the prior knowledge of students with a limited ability to comprehend complex verbal or written texts. Giving a visual example is often the only way to provide an accessible and engaging entry point for low-literacy EAL students. This also supports student participation in the whole-class brainstorming discussions. Core vocabulary that emerges from such discussions should be written down on whiteboards, on word walls and recorded in students' books or on digital learning platforms in order to assist students in retaining this information. Moving promptly between spoken and written language should be paramount in the teacher's practice. Possible strategies for activating prior learning include:

- students respond to a contentious statement or question
- watch a brief video excerpt
- students share personal anecdotes
- mindmap/ brainstorm
- students predict content from a headline or title
- use of photographs visuals, maps, diagrams and graphics
- students suggest questions to be answered on a topic
- new words written up.

Texts with embedded cultural elements that are compatible with students' own background may assist students in making connections, though this is not always possible. Inevitably in much school content, new abstract concepts are introduced that may not be immediately relevant to the students' lives. However, links can be made. For example, from the ecosystems unit mentioned earlier (McCallum & Miller, 2013b), here is a sample activity (Activity 1), that activates prior understanding on behavioural adaptations. Note also it contains terminology that will need explicit teaching and recycling for at-risk EAL students (eg, *environment, behavioural adaptation, predator*). This activity can be done prior to reading the text on adaptations.

ACTIVITY: 1

What adaptations do you know about?

Behavioural adaptations are things we do to help ourselves survive.

There are lots of things you do to help you survive in your environment.

Example: If it is very hot, I ......will have a cool drink......

This is a behavioural adaptation.

Complete the sentences below with other examples of behavioural adaptations.

If it is cold, I ....

If I feel sleepy, ...

If a bird senses danger, ...

If there is no water in a place, animals will ....

If there are lots of predators close by, animals will ....

Note that this phase of any lesson should ideally be a brief segment, something to hook students' attention, situate the topic, connect to the known and possibly flag some of the key concepts or vocabulary items.

Literal comprehension phase

Students unable to comprehend essential key content and language will struggle in all subsequent phases of learning. In other words, if you cannot understand a text, it is not possible to analyse, critique or use the text to craft a response (Miller, 2013). Therefore, the scaffolding of literal comprehension must be systematic for students who are learning new content in a new language (Cummins, 2000). If students do not understand the language of texts and tasks, they will be unable to attempt activities without individual one-to-one assistance, which is not always possible to provide in a busy classroom. It is desirable that vocabulary and meanings become part of many activities rather than be introduced by teachers at the start of a lesson. Such activities don't need to be complex or time-consuming, just regular and relevant. Suggested activities for addressing literal comprehension include:

- using visuals and real artefacts to teach vocabulary
- identifying main ideas and details
- decoding and comprehension skills
- scanning for specific information
- sequencing sections or lines of a text
- who's who (match names with roles)
- true/false questions
- note taking
- here's the answer– what's the question?
- match questions with answers
- match sentence halves
- gap fill exercises
- graphic outlines
- word walls, word banks and glossaries.

Here are two sample activities that focus on vocabulary in context: Activity 2 involves definitions and Activity 3 involves application and comprehension (Miller & McCallum, 2013b). Prior to completing these, students should have read a text on adaptations of animals in ecosystems.

ACTIVITY: 2

Identifying key vocabulary

Find these words in the text.

Use the words below to complete the sentences. Use the text to help you.

Write out a sentence that contains these words.

You can use a sentence from the text or write your own.

The first one has been done for you.

WORD	MEANING + SENTENCE
algae noun (plural)	very small organisms that live in water *There were a lot of algae in the river.*
native (adjective)	originally from a place, belonging to a place ....
organism (noun)	an animal, plant or single-celled life form ....
ecosystem (noun)	a community of organisms that interact and the environment they live in ....
interact (verb)	to have an effect on each other, work together ....
affect (verb)	to make a difference to an organism or environment ....

ACTIVITY: 3

Which verb is correct?

Choose the correct word to complete these sentences.

~~hunts~~	rises	affect
live	hides	need

Many different animals .... on the island.
The predator *hunts* its prey.
The crocodile .... in the log.
Organisms .... food and water.
The temperature .... very high.
Organisms in an ecosystem .... each other.

Comprehension in focus

Students are not able to understand what they read if even 5 per cent of the vocabulary in the text is unfamiliar to them (Nation, 2002). Students therefore need multiple opportunities to practise using new vocabulary and to apply their understanding of key concepts in different contexts. Ideally this should occur through both written and oral language activities, since these two modes are interrelated and can combine to support students towards using academic language (Gibbons, 2009b). Activities such as true/false sentences, labelling diagrams, sentence completion and gap fill exercises are examples of written tasks that scaffold student comprehension and enable teachers to monitor student understanding (Miller & McCallum, 2013b). In Activity 4 students demonstrate their comprehension of details in a text they have read. Note the systematic recycling of the key words and structures.

ACTIVITY: 4

Comprehension

Match the question and the answer. The first one is done for you.

1.................... 2.................... 3.................... 4.................... 5.....A.....

Questions	Answers
1. What animals live on the island in the picture?	A. They need them for food.
2. What is an ecosystem?	B. Non-living things like water, temperature and soil.
3. What are abiotic factors in an ecosystem?	C. Lizards, native mice and small wallabies.
4. Why do different parts of an ecosystem need each other?	D. Because they affect each other.
5. Why do birds need insects?	E. A group of living and non-living things that interact.

ACTIVITY: 5

Oral Language Task **Guess the word?**

This activity is done in small groups of up to five students.

Students stand in a circle with a chair in the middle.

Cards are placed on the chair. One student picks up a card of four words. They must try to get their team to say each of the words on the card by defining it or giving the context. They are not allowed to say the actual word, or part of it.

predator algae grow sunlight	soil arid plant photosynthesis	human nomadic environment decrease

Information gap activities, pair work and vocabulary or communication games also offer students the chance to develop their comprehension through oral language tasks. Activity 5 demonstrates how an oral language task can be used to reinforce the vocabulary and concepts of a unit.

Vocabulary activities can be embedded across a unit through short, targeted activities. Recycling the language is vital. Student retention of key vocabulary will be helped through regular quizzes where the results are recorded as diagnostic data for teachers. Even the occasional dictation may be useful. In addition, we need to teach students comprehension skills, ways to decode and to understand text, so that they are developing autonomous skills that support long-term learning. Grammar plays an important role in comprehension. Can students put the word breaks in this sentence, and what does that tell you about your students?

> *Susanlookedoveratherfriendandlaughedoutloud.*

An oral version of this is to say a sentence and ask how many words there are in it. Being able to determine word boundaries shows comprehension, knowledge of spelling and written forms, and a grasp of grammatical possibilities.

Occasions will arise when teacher explanations are needed to assist students' literal comprehension. This is particularly true in subjects where multiple meaning systems are at play. In science for example, many terms do not have the same scientific meaning as the same words in everyday language (eg *mass, model, matter*). The comprehension of low-literacy EAL students needs to be monitored in this regard. Students are unlikely to retain the technical language of mathematics or science merely by being exposed to it through text and teacher talk (Schleppegrell, 2007). A useful 'mantra' for teacher explanations is 'show don't tell.'

Critical reading and writing phase

Once students have understood the core concepts and vocabulary of a topic this enables deeper learning and more challenging cognitive work as part of the critical and creative reading and writing phase. It is important to stress that understanding 'what' precedes understanding 'how.' Cummins' (2000) transformative pedagogy model highlights the need for rich classroom interactive practice. Group work tasks where meanings are negotiated and interpretations are discussed are a vital element of student learning. Yet low-literacy EAL students may need explicit scaffolding to make this happen. Provided there is adequate support in place, students with limited language will be able to participate meaningfully in the critical and creative phase of learning, consolidating their understanding and reinforcing target language and concepts. The model suggests practice of the following aspects at this phase:

- move from oral to written activities
- grammar and structure focus

- features of text type
- joint and independent construction
- higher order thinking tasks
- creative multimodal tasks
- expressing opinions.

The critical and creative phase offers vital opportunities for low literacy EAL students to engage in higher order thinking and more cognitively challenging reading and writing tasks. The joint construction and deconstruction of texts develops student awareness of different text type features and structures. This enhances their understanding of the relationship between form, audience and purpose and improves their ability to purposefully structure their own thoughts into writing. Students may need supports such as graphic outlines, templates, subheadings or sentence starters. The table in Acrivity 6 on page 90 contains an example of scaffolding provided to assist students in writing up the results of an experiment on the interaction between colour and environment. Students looked for different coloured disks in grass, to draw their attention to the way colour adaptations can give organisms an advantage against predators.

Activities that enable students to verbalise their ideas before writing them down will be of further assistance. Pair and group work activities such as role-plays and note-taking and interviews give students the opportunity to develop content knowledge in authentic communicative contexts, before having to tackle the more challenging task of formal writing. Writing in a small group has also been shown to produce better texts than individual writing, especially for beginning writers.

Scaffolding within this phase of learning can also support students further in their reading comprehension. For example, group work tasks where students must come to a consensus encourage students to consider different interpretations of a text and look for evidence to support their opinions. There are multiple ways to incorporate critical reading and writing into classroom practice. Many of the existing models outline the importance of this phase yet do not always flag the importance of continuously attending to language recycling and expanding, the provision of comprehensible input, the scaffolding of grammar and text type structures and the inclusion of a joint construction stage. Complex and creative reading, thinking and writing rely on such activities as part of classroom practice.

Assessment phase

The diagrammatic representation of our proposed pedagogy model (Figure 6.1) views the 'assessment phase' as summative and distinct from the 'monitoring and feedback phase', which is routine ongoing evaluation of student progress that occurs continuously. The phases are not different in regards to the function of providing assessment for the purpose of planning and guiding student learning. But the assessment phase is a more

ACTIVITY: 6

INVESTIGATION: Colour adaptations Date:

Aim:

To find out ....

Method

What did you do? Use the verbs in the box to help you and complete the sentence.

~~measured~~	marked	scattered
collected	counted	recorded

1. First we .... measured out a 3m x 3m area ....
2. Then we ....
3. Then we ....
4. ....

Results

What happened? Fill in the data table below.

Colour	Number/ Not found

Conclusion

What did you learn from this experiment? Use the words in the box in your answer.

predators	camouflage	therefore	survival rate

....

....

....

formal phase, typically at the end of a unit of work, to determine the extent to which learning goals have been met, and to inform the school community.

The usefulness of these data in regards to how accurately they reflect the progress of low- literacy EAL students is dependent on a number of factors. First, teachers must ascertain whether students understood the requirements of the assessment task itself (also see Chapter 5 by Hammond in this book). It should be clear whether any errors or deficiencies in a student's work were the result of an inability to complete the task or rather a failure to understand what was expected or what was being asked. This highlights the necessity of giving clear instructions and modifying the language of the task if needed. Second, the criteria used for assessment should include content knowledge and subject-specific skills and language goals. Third, wherever possible, assessment could be modified to more accurately reflect the progress of students struggling with EAL, rather than pitting them against native speaker norms.

The following two sections, namely Language Recycling and Expanding, and Monitoring/Feedback, are critical aspects of a scaffolded literacy pedagogy rather than 'phases' of a teaching and learning cycle. Our model places them at the core, intrinsic to all other phases except summative assessment. They stem from understandings of essential second language learning principles, and from the notion of 'assessment for learning' (Hattie, 2009). There are multiple strategies for language recycling and monitoring progress, many of which can be fun and engaging. Such strategies are needed to reinforce language structures and to inform teacher planning and student awareness.

Language recycling and expanding

Low literacy EAL students need multiple opportunities to practise using new language structures. Matching new vocabulary to meanings and using words in context; completing cloze tasks; practising sentence and paragraph skills; predicting outcomes; developing comprehension and grammar skills are all essential to learning content and language. The key to the effectiveness of these tasks often lies in how prudently target language and content are integrated into the full range of learning activities. Games and role-plays are sometimes used as an engaging way for students to recycle vocabulary and negotiate content. However, these activities need a clear focus, not only on what specific content will be reinforced, but also on how the students will be supported to engage with content in a meaningful way. If students can avoid using new language in pair work for example, the activity is self-defeating. The many options for recycling and expanding language include:

- vocabulary games
- classifying activities
- transforming text to another text type (eg a news article to an email or poem)
- generating a word bank
- word–meaning match
- cloze exercises
- ICT work
- labelling diagrams
- word-building activities
- odd word out, where students justify which word does not belong

- jumbled word order (cut up sentences)
- word puzzles
- putting words in alphabetical order
- dividing up a stream letters into words.

Speaking tasks and vocabulary practice activities play an important role in the recycling and expanding phase. As previously mentioned, this is particularly true for subjects such as Mathematics, which contain a dense combination of symbols, diagrams and technical language (Schleppegrell, 2007). While group work tasks enable students to practise using subject specific language, low-literacy EAL students may need additional support to participate fully. The composition of groups can help to encourage the equal involvement of all group members. Activities that support the transference from oral to written language should also be regularly included. It has often been pointed out that a text-rich environment (visual and verbal) supports learning and this cannot be over-emphasised for these learners.

Monitoring/ feedback

In addition to summative assessment tasks at the end of each unit or topic, particularly in highly diverse classrooms, teachers need routines for monitoring whether or not students understand or have learned key aspects of the topic along the way. Knowing where students are is vital to be able to pitch lessons at the appropriate level or to strategically build on students' existing understanding and skills. Students also need to know how they are going and to have something to aim for. If monitoring is based on observational data alone, feedback to students lacks clarity and specificity (O'Neill & Gish, 2008). A positive student reaction to a task may indicate a level of comprehension. However, it could equally indicate a student's willingness to please or their desire to 'save face'.

We recommend that students' understanding and learning are monitored and recorded regularly in order to give students feedback and targeted advice on how to improve. Monitoring and feedback can be linked with teaching and learning goals, but simple means can work for this purpose, such as a quick pen-and-paper quiz, a spelling or vocabulary test, or a worksheet that is collected and marked. The positioning of the Monitoring and Feedback Phase within the inner circle of the model is significant. It indicates the need to incorporate brief monitoring tasks throughout the entire teaching and learning cycle. The process is also related to students' metacognitive understanding of themselves as learners, and of the need to set their own learning goals. Monitoring and feedback routines can include:

- peer feedback
- tests and quizzes
- worksheet completion

- homework tasks
- oral and written feedback
- observation
- recording results and comments.

Conclusion

Our language-scaffolding model proposes an intensive mode of teaching with an explicit awareness of and planning for student language acquisition and content learning. The phases of the model are integrated and interdependent, representing the dimensions of good practice rather than a rigid sequential structure. The model highlights the conditions for language learning and suggests how to meet the needs of EAL students who are still in the early phases of acquiring literacy in English. Above all, students need to be 'doing' content-based literacy work, not listening to lengthy teacher explanations, or reading texts that are too complex to be meaningful to them (McCallum & Miller, 2013a). If teachers cannot locate suitable texts and language activities, these will need to be developed. For students to work autonomously, this can be done with booklets of texts and activities or by using appropriate technology. We do not believe worksheets are a problem – bad worksheets (boring, repetitive, easy) are the problem. Challenging worksheets that force students to retrieve language and to think tend to work very well with at-risk EAL students. With increasing demands placed on teachers' time, finding innovative ways of providing intensive scaffolding across all learning areas is crucial. Aides, senior students, peers and resource sharing across whole schools and networks have the potential to achieve this.

Professional development that demystifies grammar and texts could also help teachers scaffold work for students. Through close analysis of language and texts, teachers will be able to address the complex challenges low-literacy EAL students face, and to develop a repertoire of strategies and tasks that work. Through the adoption of an integrated approach to scaffolding second language literacy, the students will be better placed to participate fully in their classrooms, and to progress alongside their mainstream peers.

Acknowledgement

The model presented in this chapter was a product of research funded by an ARC linkage grant, 'Literacy Pedagogy for refugee-background students: Connecting language, literacy and content-based learning,' (2011–13). The ARC linkage partner was the Victorian Department of Education and Early Childhood Development and chief investigators were Jenny Miller and Joel Windle. The sample unit we referred to is available on a DEECD website (McCallum & Miller, 2013b).

7

Scaffolding multimodal literacies: Learning in and out of the classroom

Karen Dooley

It is about 3:30 pm on the first Thursday of Term 2. Dana* and Brinella are two of the fourteen students gathered in the primary school library. Jessie, a musician, has just finished teaching the concept of tempo, showing the students some basic skills for operating GarageBand on their laptops, and demonstrating how to use the sampler. She is now walking around the room, monitoring the students' attempts to select and copy samples and reminding them to match the tempo of their samples. After stopping the students' work to demonstrate the effects of mismatched tempo, she says, 'You can help others if you were here before [last year]'. When the students begin work again Dana assists Brinella. After a while, Brinella says, 'Now I get it'.

This chapter suggests ways of creating digital learning environments for at-risk EAL students. It describes the experiences of Dana and Brinella at MediaClub, an afterschool digital literacy program for 12-year-olds. The club ran one afternoon a week at a primary school in a satellite city beyond the outer suburbs of an Australian state capital.

** All names used in this chapter have been changed to protect privacy*

It was one component of the URLearning (pronounced as "You are learning", hereafter designated as 'URL') research project (2010–14) which sought to develop approaches to print and digital literacy education for primary schools in high-diversity, high-poverty areas. I had a participant/observer role in the club, assisting the lead teacher and producing data for the study. In this chapter I propose that some of the pedagogic principles of MediaClub are applicable in the regular classroom and that digital literacy programs might complement the homework clubs that schools often provide to support the learning of students of refugee background.

Dana and Brinella were born in the Democratic Republic of Congo (DRC). They belong to a small Australian community comprised primarily of people who have arrived quite recently on humanitarian visas. The 2001 census identified only 270 DRC-born residents in Australia, but by 2004–05 the DRC was one of the top ten source countries of humanitarian entrants (Commonwealth of Australia, 2006). Service provision for this type of new and emerging community is complex (Government of Western Australia, 2012). While members of the DRC community bring a wealth of multilingual resources to diasporic life (Ndhlovu, 2013), high-level English literacy and academic needs are common. Moreover, success in education and other institutions may be impacted by pre-arrival trauma and medical conditions as well as post-settlement experiences of poverty, visible difference and transition to unfamiliar lifestyles (see Chapter 1). Nonetheless, there is considerable and indeed noticeable diversity within these communities. In primary schools, for instance, the language learning needs of students such as 9-year-old Brinella, who has been in Australia for 7 years, differ from those of students such as 12-year-old Dana, who has been here for 4 years.

This chapter looks at the MediaClub pedagogy that was observed and studied in terms of questions such as: What attracted Dana and Brinella to this afterschool space of learning and teaching? How might the MediaClub pedagogy connect with literacy pedagogy in mainstream primary school classrooms?

An overview of the URL project

The project was conducted in a high-diversity, high-poverty setting. The school enrolment of approximately 600 was drawn from 23 different cultural backgrounds. About 15 per cent of the students identified as Aboriginal or Torres Strait Islander. In addition, there were substantial populations of white Australians and Maori and Pacific Islanders in the school, along with small groups of migrants and refugees from around the world. About 10 per cent of the students lived in homes where English was an additional language. At the beginning of the study, about six per cent of the students were eligible for support from EAL specialists. Amongst these were students from new and emerging communities of Burmese and Afghanis, as well as Congolese. Poverty affected the lives of many of the students of all ethnic groups; the school was located in a suburb ranked amongst the lowest five per cent nationally by combined socio-economic indicators (Luke, Woods & Dooley, 2011).

The URL project entailed design-based research in both in-classroom and out-of-classroom settings in the study school. Design-based research does not merely document existing practice, but creates new practices (Mills & Levido, 2011). The in-classroom components of the URL project involved collaborative re-design of practices with teachers from Prep to Year 7, with a particular emphasis on Year 4. This component included opportunities for teachers to build their digital media skills for the new practices they were enacting in their classrooms. Much of the learning was informal and collaborative as the teachers worked alongside the media experts on the URL project; some teachers also engaged in self-directed exploration of digital media tools, building skills as they incorporated iMovie and other tools into their everyday family life. The in-classroom components of the project were part of a whole-school curriculum reform initiative. There were two out-of-classroom components. MediaClub was one, and it was designed and initially run by URL researchers. The other out-of-classroom component consisted of links to the Dreaming Circle, an afterschool learning space for Indigenous students that was supported by URL personnel (Davis-Warra, Dooley & Exley, 2011).

The MediaClub component of the URL project was designed to provide interested students from these poverty-affected communities with opportunities to learn media skills that might not otherwise have been accessible to them (Woods, Levido, Dezuanni & Dooley, forthcoming). Teachers were not initially involved in the running of the Club, although several teachers assumed responsibility for the Club at the end of the research project and worked collaboratively with the researchers during the hand-over period. URL researchers assumed that participation in the digital literacies of the everyday world is as significant an equity issue as participation in those of the formal school program (Ito et al., 2010). It was hoped that students might take skills from MediaClub to their homes and communities as well as into the digitally enriched learning activities that were being designed in classroom programs in the school.

One media production module of about 8 weeks was taught at MediaClub each term. Each module culminated in a showcase activity, such as an exhibition to which teachers, school administration and the students' families were invited. The club ran as part of the URL project for 14 terms. Module content included:

- film-making
- Lego robotics
- GarageBand
- stop motion animation
- media remix (photography, film-making and webpage-building)

- comics, digital publishing (e-books, posters, photography, film-making)
- podcasting and radio production
- video games
- macro photography
- iPad-based storytelling.

At MediaClub, when run by URL personnel, the lead teacher was sometimes the URL media teacher or a URL researcher – all of whom were involved variously in other components of the URL project. At other times, the lead teacher was an artist or musician employed for the eight afterschool sessions of the MediaClub term. At the end of the URL project an approach to MediaClub, sustainable with school-based resources, was developed with interested teachers, and responsibility for the club was handed over to the school (Woods et al., forthcoming). An account of the participation and pedagogy during the period when MediaClub was part of the URL project follows.

MediaClub participants and their motivations

MediaClub was advertised to all 9- to 12-year-old students at the school. Depending on equipment requirements for a given module, there were places for about 16–20 students each term. Interested students were expected to commit to regular attendance for the whole term.

Although not specifically for EAL learners/users or students of refugee background, in fact, many of the regulars at MediaClub were EAL students. When I mentioned Dana's and Brinella's participation to the EAL teacher during an interview, she said that Congolese parents, like others of refugee and migrant background, encouraged their children to capitalise on every opportunity for learning available to them:

> … in order to maximise the students' potential to grasp everything they can from education, if there are extra-curricular or outside-of-school-hours activities offered, you'll often find that the parents will be very supportive of their students staying on to get extra – whatever it is.

By the students' accounts, MediaClub appealed for two reasons. First, and in the words of one of the regulars, the club was '*a place for hanging out with friends*' (Woods et al., forthcoming). Dana and Brinella were no exception. For instance, when I asked Dana towards the end of the Term 2 GarageBand module why she went to MediaClub, she responded, '*to have fun, to meet new people*'. This was not an idiosyncratic response; social reasons featured in many students' answers to the same question during that round of interviews. Crucially though, digital media use seemed to be central to hanging out at MediaClub. This is not surprising: many of the worlds in which twenty first century young people like to hang out are digital (Ito et al., 2010).

Second, the students liked MediaClub for the learning opportunities it afforded. In interview after interview they spoke enthusiastically of skills and learning and teaching. Brinella's reason for attending MediaClub is indicative: '*I think it just gives me more experience because I really love singing so I think that it just gives me more experience. It can just teach you what you don't know*'. So too is Dana's reason: '*Cos we're doing different things. Cos we're learning different things*'. In other words, MediaClub was a learning space where EAL learners/users of refugee background could pursue interests and develop capabilities in digital media while hanging out with other students. But how were the students taught '*what you don't know*' at MediaClub? Why might that pedagogy be effective? To answer those questions we begin with what is known about the pedagogic conditions for optimal EAL learning.

Pedagogy and EAL learning

For EAL learners, academic success requires an extended period of language and literacy development, much of which occurs after they have been placed in mainstream classrooms. International evidence shows that it takes 5 to 7 years at best for EAL learners to reach an average level of academic language proficiency after first entering an English medium schooling system (Thomas & Collier, 1997). As was noted in Chapter 1, basic interpersonal language skills are learnt fairly quickly and easily. Indeed, some young Africans in Australia have picked up conversational skills in cross-border African languages and African Englishes both en route to and after re-settlement in Australia (Ndhlovu, 2013). In contrast, learning academic English is a far more protracted undertaking: academic achievement gaps can open up during transition into an English-medium schooling system and take a long time to resolve. It is academic English that is the source of difficulty for many learners of refugee background.

To close an initial academic gap of three years, while keeping up with grade-level peers who are learning apace in their first language, an EAL student must maintain the equivalent of one and a half years of academic progress every year for six years. For students whose schooling has been interrupted by conflict and trauma, the catch-up period is even more protracted, sometimes up to 10 years – a 'truly formidable' undertaking (Thomas & Collier, 1997, p. 46). Given that entitlement to specialist EAL support is limited to a few years, much of the responsibility for teaching during this period falls to mainstream teachers. However, this does not mean that mainstream teachers need to develop alternative programs for their students.

To clarify, in the absence of bilingual programs, EAL students are likely to progress most rapidly in English language programs that are intellectually rigorous, pedagogically engaging and socio-culturally supportive (Thomas & Collier, 1997). Such programs provide opportunities for learning English through complex, grade-appropriate content; they make use of interactive, creative and technologically engaging activities; they address language and literacy across the curriculum; they are safe spaces where linguistic and cultural difference is valued and respected. With appropriate differentiated pedagogy, EAL students can achieve academic success in these programs that would be denied them by low-challenge low-support alternatives (see Chapter 1). This ethos infused the URL project.

In the classroom-based components of the project there was an emphasis on intellectual demand, connectedness to students' worlds, sustained conversation, and extensive use of engaging digital technologies (Woods, Dooley, Luke & Exley, 2014). It is evident from relevant international literature and research that attention to basics such as phonics was needed, but would not be sufficient on its own to improve student achievement. Also, EAL students were capable of discussing complex ideas relevant to their world even while they were still learning the print basics. Internationally, refugee advocates have argued for this type of program and against impoverished programs with a singular focus on the basics of print literacy (Christie & Sidhu, 2002). Recent research provides inspiring examples – it shows how some middle school teachers have been able to create such learning opportunities while implementing the Australian Curriculum in their classrooms (Morgan et al., 2014). But this type of pedagogy can be complex to implement. When literacy pedagogy is digitalised, for example, scaffolding may become more complex.

Scaffolding for differentiation in digitalised literacy pedagogy

A recent Australian study provides insights into some of the pedagogic challenges presented by digital literacies (Simpson & Walsh, 2014). The study was conducted in a fifth grade classroom in the lead-up to the annual testing round of the National Assessment Program—Literacy and Numeracy (NAPLAN). The study teacher was exploring possibilities for embedding iPads into literacy instruction in his classroom. The unit is notable for the extensive support provided to the students. In the course of the unit, the teacher employed two different types of scaffolding: designed-in and contingent.

To clarify, designed-in scaffolding occurs during unit planning (Sharpe, 2001). It entails the selection and sequencing of experiences to help learners acquire new knowledge and skills. In the fifth grade unit (Simpson & Walsh, 2014), the teacher used several different apps to help the students learn about the persuasive genre and build content knowledge on junk food advertising. In contrast, contingent scaffolding occurs as teachers identify 'teachable moments' in the course of instruction (Sharpe, 2001). In this unit, contingent scaffolding was employed as the students were constructing their assessment piece – a multimodal junk food advertisement produced with the app version of GarageBand. Specifically, students learnt the app by exploring it and seeking assistance from teacher and peers as required.

In this fifth grade classroom (Simpson & Walsh, 2014), the sheer diversity of individual learning pathways meant that demand for contingent scaffolding became overwhelming. Further, students did not attain expected standards of mastery of the features of written persuasive texts – a source of concern given the centrality of print literacy to the looming NAPLAN assessment. At the time the teacher said that digitalisation was producing an 'overcomplicated classroom where everyone is doing their own thing to a diminished standard due to lack of pacing' (Simpson & Walsh, 2014, p. 135). By the teacher's account, quality was suffering because the student-controlled pace of learning was inadequate to the usual standard of performance. This is one of the pitfalls of digitalsation that URL project activities sought to avoid. Previous research had shown that learning time can be squandered when digital literacy pedagogy is insufficiently explicit (Mills & Levido, 2011).

The MediaClub pedagogy can be described in terms of the iPed model developed as part of the URL project (Mills & Levido, 2011). The model provides guidance for teachers as they assist students to move from text consumption to creative, collaborative text production. It emerged from participant-observation in over 180 lessons taught by the URL media teacher and the Year 4 teachers in the first years of the project. It was developed to provide pedagogic guidance for teachers in high-diversity, high-poverty schools who were seeking to move from print-oriented practices of writing education to practices consistent with authentic uses of literacy in contemporary digital worlds. It has four phases: Link, Challenge, Co-create and Share (See Figure 7.1 adapted from Mills and Levido, 2011).

Link, Challenge and Co-create are phases for designed-in scaffolding. They can be used to provide explicit instruction on hardware, software, texts and digital literacy practices. Within each of these phases contingent scaffolding may be used at teachable moments. Each phase is of value for EAL learners of refugee background.

- In the *Link* phase prior knowledge is activated. This includes students' knowledge of the world and their experience of it and of the texts and digital practices in their world. This element is especially important for negotiating the significant differences between the experiences of EAL students of refugee background and their peers in the Australian classroom.
- In the *Challenge phase* students analyse how digital texts work and the messages carried by given examples of those texts. This element involves explicit instruction in the features and purposes of texts, a long-established principle of EAL writing pedagogy (Hammond, 2001). It also involves attention to worldviews and perspectives in texts. Moreover, it attends to issues of importance in cyber worlds: online safety, democracy, censorship and intellectual property. All of this explicit instruction is of value for EAL students of refugee background who are entering new literate worlds through their everyday and schooled lives in Australia.

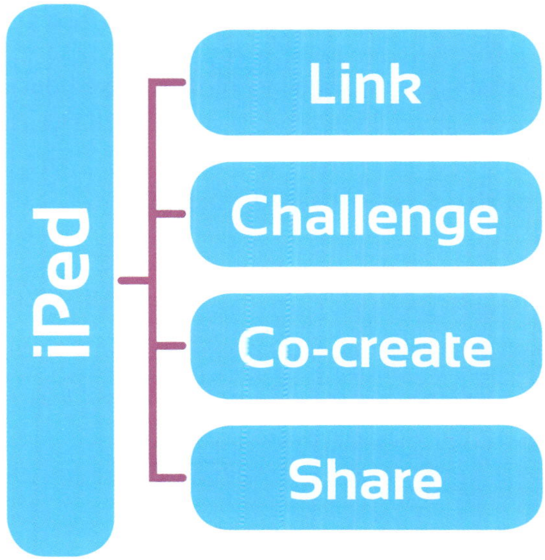

Figure 7.1: The iPed model: Instructional principles for creative, collaborative digital learning

- In the *Co-create* phase, experts scaffold novices into the production of creative multimedia texts. This element is consistent with the emphasis on scaffolding that has long been part of EAL pedagogy (Sharpe, 2001). It is assumed, further, that expertise and authority for scaffolding are not necessarily concentrated in the teacher, but may be distributed in the class. A student with high-level EAL needs, for instance, might be an expert on some aspect of digital literacy. During this phase of iPed EAL students may take on a scaffolding role during the three Co-create moves:
  - *Predict* – students speculate about purpose and function of text or software, making links to their existing knowledge and practice
  - *Demonstrate* – a student or teacher expert demonstrates some feature of text or software
  - *Do* – students try out their new knowledge in a socio-culturally supportive environment with contingent scaffolding from more expert peers or the teacher. The aim is for expertise to be 'handed over' to the learner as suggested by Brinella's comment after Dana showed her how to match the tempo of GarageBand samples: *'Now I get it'*.
- In the *Share* phase, students' media products are disseminated within and beyond the learning space to garner recognition and status in actual and virtual communities. At MediaClub sharing times were scheduled at the end of each session and a showcase session was scheduled at the end of each module. EAL students displayed their media products in both forums.

Scaffolding digital pedagogy at MediaClub

It is worthwhile here to examine how elements of iPed played out at MediaClub. The focus in particular is on the GarageBand module with which this chapter opened.

Table 7.1: Content of the GarageBand module

Week 1	Introduction to GarageBand (operation; samples; tempo)
Week 2	Editing samples (song structure; GarageBand tools; tempo)
Week 3	Adding midi instruments (introduction; playing in time; patterns)
Week 4	Music and literacy (adding words, thoughts, feelings; recording)
Week 5	Voice and instrumentation (recording)
Week 6	Consolidating works
Week 7	Mixing (volume; panning; FX, reverb, deal, eq)
Week 8	Consolidating work and burning group disc (adding track to iTunes; burning CD)

The MediaClub program of media production was carefully structured. Table 7.1 shows the content taught during the GarageBand module. This table shows that new content was introduced most weeks. An interesting feature of this pedagogy is that the students began working on their showcase piece from the outset of the module, adding to it as they learnt new things.

Each weekly workshop ran for two hours beginning as soon as school finished for the day. See Woods et al., (2014) for a description of the usual session routine. About an hour and forty minutes was devoted to teaching and learning. A sequence of three interactive routines occurred most weeks: group time, independent work time, and group sharing time. A description of each of these routines follows, illustrated with a recount reconstructed from field notes. Several URL researchers supported the musician who was the lead teacher for the module each week.

1 GROUP TIME (25 minutes)
The afternoon's tasks and expected learning outcomes were introduced by the lead teacher/s. New language and concepts were developed and new skills demonstrated.

> Jessie, the lead teacher, asked the students if they knew what 'tempo' was. Jorge said 'I know what it is but I can't explain it'. Jessie then clapped different tempos and defined the concept for the students.

> After the students logged-on to their laptops, Jessie showed them basic operational skills for GarageBand.
>
> Jessie then demonstrated how to use GarageBand samples. After that, she directed the students to begin building up their tracks by copying samples, 'Pick the beat you like and copy it; command plus C equals copy'.

In this routine Jessie made links to prior knowledge and challenged the students with a musical concept. She began co-creation by demonstrating operational and technical skills for using GarageBand.

2 INDEPENDENT WORK TIME (1 hour)
Students worked individually, in pairs or in small groups on their showcase pieces for the module, applying the skills and knowledge introduced in group time.

> As the students copied samples, Jessie went around the room monitoring their work. While doing so, she said to Dana, who was sitting with Brinella, 'You did a good one last time, I remember [from last year]'.
>
> Next, Jessie went over to Heli and Sarah, reminding them to match the tempo of their samples. She then attracted the attention of the whole class and provided an amusing demonstration of the effects of mismatched tempo. After that, Jessie reminded the more expert students to help those who were new to GarageBand, 'You can help others if you were here before [last year]'. Dana assisted Brinella. After a little while, Brinella said, 'Now I get it'.

In this routine Jessie provided a socio-culturally supportive environment as the students tried out the skills she had demonstrated. She challenged students to understand a musical concept. And she enlisted the more expert students to provide contingent scaffolding for their peers. Dana was able to scaffold the work of Brinella, a student more proficient in English but less experienced with GarageBand.

3 GROUP SHARING TIME (15 minutes)
Students showed their work to their peers and teachers for feedback and/or the lead teacher/s provided group feedback.

I have no observations illustrating this routine from the Week 1 session. From my two years at MediaClub, I can, however, make some general comments. First, no student was ever compelled to share their work. Second, students were reinforced for identifying both strengths and weaknesses in their work and offering constructive feedback on the work of their peers. Third, students were encouraged to use technical language when talking about their work. Fourth, students were told how the next week's workshop would enhance their developing project.

> In this routine the students received more-or-less immediate recognition for their learning from the adults and the peers with whom they hung out at MediaClub. Students were expected to use the challenging knowledge and skills they had acquired and preparation was made for further cycles of challenge and co-creation. The purposes of learning were made explicit and skill development was linked clearly to the students' project work – the piece they were producing for the end-of-term Showcase.

This example demonstrates that MediaClub pedagogy required the students to begin producing the track they would eventually burn to the group CD from the very first week of the module. The tracks were built up cumulatively over the weeks as each new skill was introduced. The MediaClub pedagogy, as noted in the field notes, enabled a '*gradual build-up of technical skills, language and product*' over the course of the module. In this note 'technical skills' is a catch-all term that includes knowledge of musical concepts (eg, tempo) and expertise in using GarageBand features to produce music (eg, the sampler). This pedagogy was typical of what I observed during the two years of research at MediaClub.

Each week of the GarageBand module, Jessie used the same sequence of interactive routines. First she provided explicit instruction for the whole group (the concept of tempo, operating GarageBand, using the sampler) and then she directed the students to apply what they had learnt to their own Showcase piece. This was consistent with the scaffolding approach of the iPed model. The session always ended with a sharing phase.

In Week 5 of the GarageBand module, one of the researchers, a media teacher, overtly discussed the principles of MediaClub pedagogy with the students. At the beginning of independent work time that day, the students had not been engaged as deeply as usual in their projects. In intervening the teacher tried to explain the pedagogic logic of the module to them. He sought to shift the students' understanding of how learning proceeds, reframing doing the same thing every week as a pedagogic necessity:

> ... [the] whole point is that you learn something new each week. So don't just play around a bit with what you did last week. It's ok if [your] lyrics [are] not good today. [The] whole process of writing lyrics, and recording and adding to it is very important.

From the teacher's comments it is clear that the ideal MediaClub learner returns to their project week after week, adding to it as they acquire new knowledge and skills. Persistence is important; a weak song can be improved over time. For this reason, a token effort is not acceptable.

The engagement difficulties of Week 5 were the exception. Field notes for the GarageBand module are studded with comments such as '*engagement really high*'. As a teacher with many years' experience and a researcher who has clocked up hundreds of hours of classroom observation, I was struck by the level of engagement.

Like most of their peers were most of the time, Dana and Brinella were usually absorbed by MediaClub activity. About an hour into the Week 7 workshop, for example, Brinella was watching the teacher's demonstration of distortion with '*absolute attention*'. She was one of four students listening intently to the teacher's explanation; the other students were '*at work alone*' on their projects or '*quietly talking*' [about their work, I thought] with peers. Dana was likewise observed to be engaged during the MediaClub workshops answering teacher questions during group time, helping Brinella in response to the teacher's suggestion, and working with absorption alongside peers in a small group.

In summary, the GarageBand module entailed scaffolding by which the students cumulatively built up a media product, in this case, a song for burning to a group CD at the end of term. All the principles of iPed were in evidence. Links were made to prior knowledge; students were challenged with musical concepts; and expert instruction and contingent scaffolding were provided as students co-created their products (Mills & Levido, 2011). The products were shared at the end of each session and by the burning and distribution of the group CD at the end of the module, thereby enabling the learners to take on identities as multimedia producers. Brinella enjoyed particular acclaim in this iPed phase the following term when the I-movie she had made with a friend was featured at a showcase event to which parents, friends and school staff had been invited. Brinella provided a brief oral introduction to the movie and then played it for the audience. She had been coached for this role by the lead teacher and had opportunities to practise her oral presentation. In short, Dana and Brinella, like all the MediaClub students, seem to have been engaged by the pedagogy. Moreover, there was evidence of digital literacy learning.

Student learning at MediaClub

From Table 7.1 it can be seen that Jessie taught the students three strands of content. One entailed operational skills for GarageBand software. Another focused on oral and written literacy required for the song, for example, '*adding words to express thoughts and feelings*'. Most of the module, however, focused on audio meaning-making, specifically, how to use GarageBand features.

To get some insights into what Brinella and Dana learnt from the GarageBand module, it is useful to look at the interviews conducted with the girls towards the end of the module. When interviewed, Brinella provided a detailed account of her learning, some of which follows:

KD *What did you learn at MediaClub today?*

B *I learned about, I didn't know about tempo. I didn't know like, if you have to, if your music was too loud it make it like, destruction, I think it was*

KD *Distortion*

B *Distortion and she just taught us a lot and I didn't really like know how to make music and how they did it and yeah, stuff like that.*

By her own account, Brinella was learning technical skills (eg, avoiding distortion) and seems to have been acquiring relevant metalanguage ('tempo', 'distortion'). These were learnings she valued. It will be recalled that Brinella loved singing and saw MediaClub as an opportunity to be taught things she did not know. Avoiding distortion was only one of the skills Brinella went on to discuss in the interview. It was a skill that Brinella could envisage taking back to the classroom.

KD: *Is there anything you learnt this afternoon or in other weeks that you can take back to the classroom?*

B: *Cos in our classroom we're recording ballads so I can like show them all the distortions and stuff.*

Later in the interview Brinella described the ballad unit in detail. In doing so, she said that she and a friend who had attended MediaClub the year before could use their MediaClub skills to help the class record a ballad. Brinella was also able to envisage taking her MediaClub skills home. She spoke of teaching her sister, who also loved music, the skills she was learning at MediaClub. This was consistent with our goal of providing students with opportunities to become digital experts in their everyday and schooled worlds.

In contrast, Dana said that she had not learnt anything new on the day of the interview. In response to a direct question from me about her learning that day she replied: *'I don't know, cos all of them [the things we learned today], I have done, yes, I done last year'*. When interviewed by another researcher during the previous year's GarageBand module, Dana said that she had learnt about the spacing between samples. In bringing knowledge and skill from that GarageBand module to the current one, Dana too was able to take on the role of a digital expert. But how might this learning, achieved in an afterschool space, connect with literacy education in the mainstream classroom for EAL learners of refugee background?

Connections to literacy education in mainstream classrooms

Mainstream programs, we are arguing in this book, can be taught in ways that provide productive learning environments for EAL students at risk. Those programs, however, need to be intellectually rigorous, pedagogically engaging and socio-culturally supportive. In conclusion let us look at ways that activities such as MediaClub might be connected with the mainstream literacy education program to enable the creation of such programs.

The pedagogy of MediaClub illustrates some ways of addressing the increase in demand for scaffolding that arises in differentiated and digitalised pedagogy (Simpson & Walsh, 2014). MediaClub pedagogy, like that of in-classroom URL activities, was explicit during moment of challenge and co-creation in particular. This is consistent with principles that have long been used to enable EAL learners to learn to write print genres (Hammond, 2001). Explicitness enables learners whose experience of text and literacy is most distant from that of schooled literacy to acquire mastery of powerful textual features and practices. Moreover, by positioning students as potential experts, the MediaClub pedagogy tapped into the breadth of expertise available for the scaffolding required by this pedagogy.

The MediaClub experience suggests that it is worth capitalising on the digital expertise that students might bring to the literacy classroom. This expertise is more than prior knowledge for individual understanding; it might be used as a resource for the class and in the classroom. 'Media expert' roles might be created for students in the classroom to formalise those roles. In some settings, it is possible to rely on the expertise that students bring from technologically rich homes. That was not always the case at a school in a high-poverty area. However, that expertise could be developed within the school but beyond the mainstream classroom. Many schools now run homework clubs for the most at-risk learners, afterschool activities, that is, that are directly related to the formal school program. An activity such as MediaClub is also worth consideration (see Woods et al., forthcoming, for suggestions about setting up such an activity).

Importantly for the purposes of this book, EAL learners/users, including those of refugee background, made extensive use of MediaClub and engaged with the learning opportunities available to them. This is cause for consideration. A UK study (MacBeth et al., 2001) involving more than 8000 students from 52 schools found that young people from ethnic minority groups participated more and benefited most from afterschool programs, including aesthetic activities that were not tightly linked to classroom activities (eg, Music Club, Art Club, Dance Club, African Drumming Club). Benefits went beyond knowledge and skills. They included favourable attitudes to school, better attendance and improved self-regulation in both leisure and more formal learning. In short, an aesthetic afterschool activity like MediaClub can complement the formal school literacy education program in both direct and indirect ways for EAL learners.

Acknowledgement

This chapter reports data collected as part of an Australian Research Council-funded project. I acknowledge with gratitude the *MediaClub* students and families, volunteers, artists, assistants and teachers. I thank the teachers, students and administrators at the school and the parents and Indigenous elders. I also acknowledge my research colleagues Vinesh Chandra, John Davis, Beryl Exley, Katherine Doyle, Michael Dezuanni, Amanda Levido, Allan Luke, Kathy Mills, Wendy Mott and Annette Woods of Queensland University of Technology and John McCollow and Lesley MacFarlane of the Queensland Teachers Union.

8

Classroom strategies for teachers and EAL learners

Jennifer Miller

> 'The limits of my language mean the limits of my world.'
>
> *Ludwig Wittgenstein (Philosopher, 1889–1951)*

This book has provided a detailed overview of at-risk EAL learners, their needs, challenges and some ways teachers can best teach them in mainstream classrooms.

For many of these learners, disrupted education and limited first language literacy impact heavily on their efforts to learn a new language and *through* a new language. For a child, as Uptin points out in Chapter 3, a gap in school is a 'gap in life'. Teachers cannot change the difficult past lives that many of these students have experienced, but they *can* shift their pedagogy to maximise engagement and participation so that academic success is a real possibility for all. The purpose of this chapter is to present a detailed practice-based response to teaching language and content in the mainstream curriculum. To some extent the chapter complements Chapter 6 by Miller and McCallum and its model of literacy pedagogy, however here I draw more broadly on my thirty years of experience both as language teacher and learner, and as a researcher.

Chapter 4 by Coleman and Chapter 5 by Hammond demonstrated that, overall, teachers are good at providing an accepting and supportive classroom environment – and this is extremely important. But teachers have a dual role here, namely to provide a safe and nurturing classroom, and also to raise the bar in their pedagogy to respond to the needs of their most at-risk students. To maximise participation and engagement by students, the starting point for teaching is a close understanding of the students themselves and what they bring to the learning table. This is briefly discussed in the next section, followed by a discussion of supportive classrooms and pedagogical practices that integrate language, literacy and content. An example of possible strategies using a sample text is also given. Finally, implications for further progress in this field are suggested.

What the students bring

Students from diverse backgrounds arrive at school with diverse cultural experiences, complex lives and identities, knowledge of other languages, a willingness to learn, hidden talents and interests, and a resilience often learned the hard way. Cranitch in Chapter 2 provides a vivid picture of the difficult experiences in refugee camps, which many students have known. Not all at-risk EAL students have refugee backgrounds, of course. Many factors place a child at risk, including having poor uneducated parents, living in precarious home situations, being subject to neglect or having onerous family responsibilities. For these learners, organising books, handouts, stationery, remembering things, doing homework, bringing back forms, turning up on time, and classroom routines are all new and difficult aspects of school. Recently arrived learners may also be encountering print literacy for the first time.

In Australian schools, students have to catch up with mainstream peers who have been learning intensively since preschool about texts, books, images, concepts, technology and discipline-related language and genres. What EAL students bring with them is a keystone in what Gibbons (2009b) calls 'Learning in the challenge zone'. She stresses that the way teachers think about students has a far greater impact on classrooms than they perhaps realise. Ideally teachers need to view the learners 'as the people they can become, not simply learners with limited English' and 'see a culturally diverse classroom as a resource, not a problem' (p. 166). Overall, this book has provided five clear messages for teachers. They are in one sense the conditions that enable good teaching.

1. It is important to question assumptions about what students know or understand, and to be open to having our views, as teachers, challenged.
2. The backgrounds, willingness, knowledge, talents, identities, and interests of students can be primary resources for effective language and literacy teaching. Valuing students' prior knowledge, including their linguistic knowledge and culture pays off in lessons.
3. Content and language need to be integrated in ways that make tasks accessible to learners.
4. Seeking and recognising abilities in areas outside of obvious print literacy, such as drawing, music, or dance, can be used as a springboard to literacy.
5. Developing tangible records of student work demonstrates and values progress, and shows 'what learning looks like' for students and their families.

All five 'messages' are fundamental in establishing a supportive learning environment focused on possibilities not limitations, on heightened expectations and belief in the students' abilities to think, to learn, to be readers and writers.

Because students may have limited English, initially it may be difficult for teachers to learn what interests, abilities, experiences and passions students might have. But my experience of teaching for many years in Queensland suggests there are ways to open up opportunities in classrooms, where student identities can emerge, language connections be made and talents revealed. As both Uptin in Chapter 2 and Dooley in Chapter 7 suggest, one way of doing this is to incorporate extracurricular activities into the curriculum (music and singing, art, dance, gardening, technology). It is important that teachers realise this is not another unhelpful binary. They may well ask themselves – Do I focus on language and literacy OR experiential learning, rich tasks and extracurricular activity? What is needed is not either, but *both*!

EAL teachers in intensive new-arrivals programs know that experiences are brought to life through language, and that experience and language have a vital reciprocal relationship. As a teacher, I recall one student, a quiet Taiwanese boy, Leo, who in one lesson completed an amazing pencil drawing on an A3 sheet of the entire two-storey school in perspective, from an imagined elevated position. Classrooms, landscaping and playgrounds (with students playing) were clearly defined. His classmates and I were stunned by the cleverness of the image, its attention to detail and its skill. That drawing was photocopied and hung on the classroom wall, in the school library, and in my home office. The validation of Leo's identity and ability in drawing was a transformative moment. He was happy to talk about the image, and gained new confidence in speaking and taking risks in front of other students. Finding students' talents can be a way in to language and literacy, and give a huge confidence boost that aids learning.

Supportive classrooms for these learners

What seems clear from several studies in this book is that for at-risk students, nurturing environments are not enough to generate literacy learning or academic gains. That is, for better outcomes, stronger EAL-informed pedagogy is needed. What can teachers do to teach language, literacy and content more effectively? Chapters 6 and 7 provided some specific ideas about this. It now remains to distil a useful summary for teachers to work from, and towards. In broad terms, this book has stressed the importance of classrooms and schools characterised by high challenge and high support for all learners. But this can mean many things for many different students. High challenge for one might be writing a convincing argument, while for another it may be writing three simple sentences about themselves. The ideas and strategies in this chapter assume challenge and support as a core principle. So what does this kind of classroom look like? What practices are in evidence in such classrooms?

The nature of supportive classrooms for at-risk EAL learners

1. It is a truism to say we have to walk before we run. At-risk EAL learners need an environment which acknowledges their particular *Zone of Proximal Development* (ZPD), a space where the work is actually achievable, pitched a little beyond them but still doable with some teacher support. For example, a 'learnable' text is a comprehensible text, and so it is important to ensure that texts are accessible to the students, and that understanding will not need to rely on laborious explanations by the teacher. Success builds confidence to tackle the next level of difficulty.
2. Supportive teachers have high expectations of their students, including those just beginning to 'walk'. They look at learning as an intellectual endeavour, and know that work has to be cognitively challenging and inherently interesting.
3. These classrooms are full of lively and rich interactions and meaningful communication, in which students are gently pushed beyond the bounds of normal social speech to a more informed and 'academic' talk that will help them move towards academic literacy. Their teachers say, *Can you say a bit more about that? Can you think of a better word for that? Make a longer sentence. Tell me again, I need to understand.*
4. Supportive classrooms are full of students *doing* things: working, reading, writing, drawing, analysing, viewing, creating, discussing, performing, and rehearsing. We don't learn to play tennis by listening to someone explain the physics of a ball bouncing off a racket. We become literate by engaging with language, and by using it constantly in multiple ways. For EAL students, as for all of us, the most powerful way to learn is by doing.
5. Supportive English teachers love language, are curious about how it works, and very often are readers and writers themselves. This love and curiosity are passed on to their students.
6. Linking language and content to lived experience and the students' identities is vital. Classrooms can reflect this via photographs, word walls, wonderful visuals, artefacts and technology.
7. These classrooms are often part of supportive whole-school programs, and connected to their broader communities, so that the outside world is brought into the classroom and is part of the language and literacy endeavour. Parents, volunteers and colleagues are welcome.

The practices of supportive teachers of at-risk EAL students

There are many things one could list as the practices of effective practitioners for EAL learners – each of them entailing multiple subskills or micro-practices. For example, the terms 'planning' or 'scaffolding' are broad overarching practices, but they need to be broken into diverse moves and strategies to be of practical use to teachers. Table 8.1 lists some key practices for teaching language, literacy and content to students, along with associated strategies or examples. They align with aspects of the literacy model presented in Chapter 6, though are more general in nature. The practices include planning, explicit language focus, meaning focus, literacy scaffolding, language recycling, the speaking-writing connection, and monitoring.

All of the practices listed in Table 8.1 are helpful for struggling EAL learners. Clearly no teacher could do all of this every lesson, and of course each strategy could be expanded, explained in detail and practised. It is important to try new things, to see what works with your context and your students. As a general principle, intellectual challenge, support and enjoyment are not just important – they are the key to engagement in literacy and learning. But keep in mind that while the genres and tasks of the mainstream are important, in the early stages for these learners, the genre or the text are less important than starting from where your students actually are at. In 1968, the renowned educational psychologist Ausubel wrote, 'The most important single factor influencing learning is what the learner already knows' (Ausubel, 1968, p. 18). If you have chosen a text that is funny, amazing, beautiful, curious, fascinating or extraordinary *and* accessible – students are likely to want to dive in and read it, and to use it for a whole range of writing tasks.

Table 8.1: Practices that support At Risk EAL students

Practice	Strategy or example
Planning	• Link texts and activities to mainstream curriculum. • Select texts with a view to relevance, motivation and intellectual challenge. It is better to find a readable text than to modify one, but you may need to simplify structures and vocabulary, or enlarge fonts and reduce length for some students. • Locate visuals and artefacts to bring texts and concepts to life. • Identify target language structures, vocabulary or text features to focus on. • Design tasks, activities and practice worksheets. • Plan for formative and summative assessment • Design pair, group and individual activities to make some self-directed work possible for all • Use volunteers or aides wherever possible for groups • Collaborate with colleagues to share topics and load

Practice	Strategy or example
Explicit language focus	• Genre features • Grammar and its metalanguage • Vocabulary and spelling • Pronunciation • Formulaic phrases which can be memorised • Word building (morphology) • Word games
Meaning focus	• Choose relevant and meaningful texts • Use visuals • Connect meaning to lived experience • Check comprehension through meaning matches, matching sentence halves, true/false, gap-fill tasks, and so on • Guess meaning from context • Practice using dictionaries • Focus on comprehension cues • Put meaning, risk-taking and communication before accuracy in the early phases of learning • Consider how contexts change meanings
Literacy scaffolding	• Start from prior knowledge, a concrete example, a link to the known • Build in small staged steps for those who need it • Move systematically between oral and written tasks • Use student input to do joint constructions • Build in comprehension and vocabulary tasks (in context), then move to more critical and creative work • Use visuals and hands-on activities • Provide formats such as graphic outlines, sentence starters, concept maps
Language recycling (or message abundancy)	• Give students repeated opportunities to encounter and practise new language (word and sentence level tasks; puzzles; oral summaries; group writing; dictionary work; daily recaps or pen and paper quiz; homework tasks; word walls; personal glossaries) • Write new words from oral interactions on the board – discuss them, or link them to other words • Use ICT and software programs to reinforce new language • Transform a text to a new genre, using similar language (letter to a poem; news report to an email) • Consciously use new language and provide opportunities for students to practise
The move from oral to written language	• At-risk EAL students generally have spoken English. The urgent need is for them to read and write. Ensure lessons shift from talk to reading and writing in a timely manner. • Avoid having students listening or speaking for extended periods; get them back to their desks to write or type something, or to read with a purpose.
Monitoring and feedback	• Record notes on student progress to inform your own planning and differentiation, as well as feedback to students. Use quick routine 'tests' or quizzes, collect worksheets and homework, note levels of group participation, have students self-assess or peer assess. Have them build a portfolio of work they are proud of • For summative evaluation, ensure students understand the purpose and language of the task – scale back if needed.

Figure 8.1: Water features on Cairns esplanade

The more they dive in, the more they read and write (in any form), the stronger will be their foundation for mainstream literacy. Texts do not have to be lengthy or difficult to generate plenty of language use and learning. Here is a simple example.

Water, rules and having fun

These strategies and activities are aimed at students with good basic oral skills, but limited written skills. The text is visual (Figure 8.2 on page 116), combining words and symbols. Activities are suggestions only, with many variations possible. Although the text chosen has 'minimal' language, teachers will see that there are numerous possibilities for literacy development and engagement.

The **planning** involved was to select the photos from my photo library (Figure 8.1), create a vocabulary crossword using an online puzzle maker tool (Figure 8.3 on page 117), identify target language and devise spoken and written tasks which include pair, group and individual work. Teachers could also reproduce the text icons without labels.

Target language included:

Vocabulary: esplanade; feature; littering; obey; pollute; pollution

Language for giving reasons: because, is/are not allowed to; should; have to; justified

Figure 8.2: Rules for water features

Table 8.2: Water text activities

Strategy	Activity	Comment
Activate prior knowledge	Look at photo of water features (Figure 8.1) only. Ask: *Where is this?* *What is it?* *Who might go there?* *What rules might there be for using this place?*	Link to experience. Ensure it is the students doing the talking. Make notes on the whiteboard. It is important for students to *see* key words and phrases.
Reading	Students read the Rules text (Figure 8.2). Check comprehension by miming the items (eg no littering) and see if students respond with the rule.	Talk points: *How many rules are there?* *Is 'no babies' a rule?* *What CAN you do here?*
Giving reasons for rules	Model and write up: You are not allowed to litter because this could pollute the water. Practise 2–3 more. In pairs, they are given 4 icons and have to write the rule and the reason in full sentences. ALL students to write all sentences.	Grammar focus (*are not allowed; can't; should not*) + practise at sentence level. Chance to teach one or two new words – *hygienic, pollution; dangerous, injury* For homework, they could match rules and reasons (worksheet needed). Individual writing is needed to ensure all students practise structures for giving reasons. Repeating the structure is good, and also entails different vocabulary and reasons.

Strategy	Activity	Comment
Class discussion	Why do we have rules?	Higher order thinking. If some students don't speak much in whole class talks, try this in groups. They should always make notes.
Crossword	(See Figure 8.3)	Recycling target words; language practice; thinking, definitions and spelling. Test recall of meanings and spelling the next day (and next week).
Writing task	Do one or more: a Write a paragraph about the Cairns water features and rules. Include your opinion about whether the rules are a good idea. Draw your favourite rule icon. b Think of another context. Make a list of rules for it. c A safety officer at the water features sees a child eating a banana in the water. Write the conversation.	Adds drawing as an element. Use technology if available.
Creative task	Group poster Illustrated poem – *Water* Mindmap – *Water*	All entail cognitive and language challenge, and have an aesthetic aspect as part of text.

Fun in the water

Across

4. These must keep to the cycle path
7. A place along the water's edge
9. Water.........
10. Found on beaches
11. This is bad for your health

Down

1. Pets that can't join in here
2. Do what is asked
3. Worn by babies
5. Pull yourself up or walk upwards
6. Dropping papers and containers
8. Ideas to help organise people and things

[Answers: bicycles, esplanade, feature, sand, smoking, dogs, obey, nappies, climb, littering, rules]

Figure 8.3: Fun in the water crossword puzzle

It is important to note that even in seemingly simple tasks, for example giving a reason for not drinking from glass in a water area, there is real cognitive work. Putting an idea into a new language, so that it is fluent and reasonably accurate is a high-challenge task for many students. Extending academic oral language is also part of the work suggested in Table 8.2. For some students, 'You are not allowed to ride a bike in the water area because it is dangerous for young children' might be the longest sentence they have ever uttered in English! Encourage this, ask them to use a longer sentence whenever possible. Teachers may see many other possibilities for linking to more demanding texts as part of a topic or unit. Where might those two photos take you and your students?

In conclusion – some implications

Each experienced teacher, especially those working in primary schools, may have other practices which they have tried and validated over time to help their students become readers and writers, and to enjoy the process. But many mainstream teachers facing increasing numbers of at-risk EAL students are unsure what to do. What works for students fluent in English with age-appropriate schooling does not work for these students, who are at-risk because they are emergent users of spoken English, have little or no literacy, have had disrupted education, difficult backgrounds, and are often socially disadvantaged and living in poverty or in fractured families. They will need endless chances to read and practise written forms (without being tedious) and tasks. They enjoy language games, which in tandem with in-depth text work, can provide opportunities to revise, learn and have fun.

One problem currently in Australia is that pre-service teacher education courses generally do not train primary or secondary teachers in these language-focused skills, understandings and competencies, or indeed in the cultural and social aspects of highly diverse classrooms. As a consequence, there is a pressing need for ongoing professional development in these areas for mainstream teachers of these students. This was a major finding of studies by Hammond 2014a and McCallum & Miller 2013a, and many previous studies. How can schools identify where their needs lie in terms of professional learning in this regard?

It is useful to consider briefly the kinds of specific knowledge and skills needed by students and their teachers in classrooms that are both challenging and supportive for EAL language and literacy learning. While not an exhaustive list, these are summarised in Table 8.3.

Table 8.3: Language and learning knowledge and skills

Student knowledge	Teacher knowledge
• literacy • numeracy • school routines • ICT skills • cultural meanings • organisational skills • comprehension skills • higher order thinking skills • metalinguistic awareness • content • vocabulary • concepts • connections to life experience • curriculum links	• content being taught • students' backgrounds and prior learning • how to select and modify text if needed • importance of valuing student identities • role of high expectations • planning skills • linguistic knowledge (grammar, morphology, relationship of oral to written language) • language analysis • second language and literacy principles • language and conceptual demands of texts and content • text analysis skills • scaffolding techniques • differentiation techniques • resources and ICT

The Australian Curriculum contains the phrase, 'Literacy is not simply about knowledge and skills'. Most teachers understand and support the kinds of complexity the curriculum is describing, the focus on literacy as a social practice, the need to move towards comprehending and composing a range of complex texts. But I wish to make two points based on both my research and teaching experience. First, 'comprehending and composing a range of complex texts' is not where it begins for at-risk students, and second, there is nothing simple about knowledge and skills, as you see from the table above. In fact, they are essential foundations for literacy, language development and learning.

Research tends to show that whole-school programs to support EAL learners are most effective. That is, what supports at-risk learners is also good for the wider student body as a whole. This is because in one sense, 'academic English' is nobody's mother tongue. It would be difficult for teachers to begin to implement the kinds of practices we describe independently, and so a whole-school commitment to a language and literacy approach for these learners is desirable. Peer observations, collaborative work, targeted planning time, and the search for and acquisition of inspiring print and ICT resources needs to be part of this commitment. Whole-school programs also ask that teachers reflect and 'theorise' what they are doing and why. Clearly none of this is simple or straightforward, and hence the ongoing need for targeted professional learning on language, along with the study of 'school English' as an additional language, scaffolding strategies and pedagogical practices more generally.

Before concluding this chapter on classroom pedagogy, it is important to acknowledge the powerful role played by teachers and schools in recognising and confronting the presence of racism of any kind and whenever it occurs. For some students, experiences of racist taunts made by their peers becomes yet another hurdle to overcome as they struggle to learn. Students interviewed by Uptin (Chapter 3) drew attention to the racism they perceived on almost a daily basis in their schools. They did not want to be called 'refugees,' or to have their backgrounds viewed as part of some problem. However, the fact of just looking different was very real for them, and had the consequence of drawing unwanted attention and comment. That is, physical difference impacted on the way they felt they were perceived. One student, Gabriella, concluded that, *'if you look white, you are not seen as different'*. A related finding can be found in the student voices of Miller's (2003) study, namely, that if you sound like an Aussie, you are not seen as different. Visible difference and audible difference mark EAL students in a way that can threaten their learning, progress and wellbeing. Currently in Australia, we live in a climate of heightened suspicion of refugees, asylum seekers and all those who appear or sound different. Teachers need to be the face of welcome in the Australian community – and to get this message to their Anglo-Australian students. That is, classrooms should be places where no one is judged by the way they look or sound, a lesson for *all* students to learn.

It is hoped that schools and teachers will see value in some of the ideas offered here, as a way of catering to the needs of their at-risk EAL learners. These students are resilient, keen to learn, and like all children, validated by success in learning. It is our duty to give them work they can succeed at, to become literate speakers, readers and writers, and to scaffold them towards becoming autonomous learners in the mainstream curriculum.

9

Lessons learned and ways forward

Jennifer Hammond

This book has prioritised needs of EAL students who, because of previous experiences of disruption or trauma in their lives, or because of minimal access to formal schooling prior to arrival in Australia, are likely to be 'at risk' of educational failure. As explained in Chapter 1, the overall concern of the book has been with educational successes and challenges experienced by these students and by the teachers who work with them. It has been organised around three main aims:

- to address the (diverse) needs of at-risk students within the context of mainstream classes,
- to focus on teaching and learning practices that are most likely to support students to engage equitably with the full curriculum
- to propose ways forward in the teaching of academic language and literacy across the curriculum, and in doing so, to complement and connect with the Australian Curriculum.

Chapters in the book have addressed these aims in various ways. They have also addressed the issue of equity in education. As indicated, authors share the view that equitable educational programs need to aim high, but they also need to provide very high levels of targeted support for their at-risk students. The reality of what these principles of high challenge and high support mean for teachers working with at-risk students has been a major and recurring theme across the chapters.

A number of related themes relevant to equitable education of at-risk EAL students have also emerged from the chapters. These include:

- the importance of knowing students
- the importance of students' learning environment
- teaching and learning practices in focus
- suggestions for ways forward.

What lessons can we take from chapters of this book in relation to these themes, and what implications can we draw for the education of at-risk EAL students?

The importance of knowing students

It is, of course, stating the obvious to say that teachers need to know their students. Educators and teachers are very familiar with the argument that effective education programs need to start from where students 'are at', and build from there. However, for teachers working with at-risk students, learning about your students and understanding what they bring to formal education in Australia is not always a straightforward issue. A common request from teachers is for more information about their students: about their backgrounds; their life and educational experiences prior to arrival in Australia; their knowledge of languages (their mother tongue and other languages); and their knowledge of literacy in any language. In Chapters 2 and 3, both Cranitch and Uptin address the issue of getting to know students: the kind of general information about students' cultures and languages that will assist teachers to better understand students and the kinds of adjustments required of them in Australian schools, as well as knowledge of individual students that will assist teachers to understand specific strengths and needs.

A recurring theme across initial and later chapters is that at-risk students have diverse backgrounds and needs. As Cranitch and Uptin point out, students arrive at school with a diversity of cultural experiences, complex lives and identities, and diverse knowledge of languages. Some have had extensive prior education others have not. Cranitch provides a vivid picture of the difficulties that many students have experienced prior to arrival in Australia. Her case-study accounts from refugee camps in Jordan and on the Thai/Myanmar border highlight the hazards of students' journeys and the many life challenges they have faced. Even when students have had access to education in refugee camps, the quality of that education is questionable: students were often taught by unqualified teachers in large classes where their education consisted mostly of copying or simple decoding. Cranitch also highlights the 'language soup' that is the reality for many students as they move from their home country, to one or more countries of first asylum, and finally to Australia. The result is that while some at-risk students may have conversational fluency in several languages, they may have minimal literacy in any language.

The chapters highlight the importance of knowing students and of knowing what they bring to the classroom (as well as what they do not bring). Yet for teachers, the process of getting to know their students can be challenging. Knowledge of individual students' backgrounds and their educational experiences will clearly assist in processes of program planning. However, as Miller points out, students' levels of English may limit possible conversations between teachers and students, and hence limit opportunities for teachers to learn more about these students. In addition, Uptin highlights the need for teachers to be sensitive to the possibility of reawakening past experiences of trauma, and suggests that teachers may need to take an indirect approach to discussions about students' past lives. Cranitch argues that knowing students also involves knowing about their cultures and languages. She encourages teachers to question their own assumptions about what students know or understand, and to be open to having their views challenged. She also suggests that teachers make use of available information about immigration processes, as well as general background information about students' countries of origin, cultures, schooling, and languages. (Refer to the list of Useful websites at the end of the book.)

The adjustment required of students when they begin school in Australia is substantial, and a number of authors address this issue. When at-risk EAL students arrive at school in Australia, they are faced with learning social and academic English, gaining cultural understandings, learning content knowledge and concepts, and catching up with mainstream peers who have been learning intensively since preschool about texts, books, images, concepts, technology and discipline-related language and literacy. Despite the scale of this challenge, students' own resources provide a solid basis for teachers to work with. In earlier chapters, Cranitch, Uptin and Hammond all emphasise students' strengths: their skills, talents and dispositions, their musical and sporting abilities, their resilience, energy and determination, and their humour. All chapters in the book emphasise the importance of knowing where students 'are at', of connecting with students' background knowledge and of building on this in the design and implementation of educational programs

The importance of students' learning environment

While the major focus of the book as a whole is its emphasis on the kinds of pedagogical practices that are most likely to support at-risk EAL students in mainstream classes, all authors make the point that without a supportive and safe learning environment, students will not be in a position to engage with school learning. This is especially the case for those who have experienced major disruptions, and possibly trauma, prior to their arrival in Australia. A positive and supportive learning environment is a necessary prerequisite for effective learning, and all authors acknowledge its pivotal role in the education of at-risk EAL students.

As a number of the chapters make clear, many schools and individual teachers are well aware of the importance of learning environments. Many schools already have in place a range of programs and strategies that enable at-risk (and other) students to feel safe, valued and supported. Some of these programs are specifically oriented to students' welfare, while others intersect and overlap with supportive pedagogical practices. Hammond in Chapter 5 for example, describes whole-school programs that welcomed students and assisted them to feel part of the school community; that addressed relevant welfare issues, and assisted students with cultural adjustments; and that addressed issues of racism and bullying. Such programs helped students adjust to the new cultural environment of school in Australia. She also described programs provided by EAL specialist teachers that supported students' academic learning and their language and literacy development. Some of these were implemented in parallel English classes and others were implemented in conjunction with mainstream subjects. Such programs supported students in academic work, and encouraged them to envisage a future for themselves at school and into their future in Australia.

At the classroom level, both Hammond and Coleman reported evidence that individual teachers were particularly strong in providing, supportive and inclusive learning environments for all students, including at-risk EAL students. From her primary school research, Coleman reported classroom environments where students felt safe and respected, and where their teachers cared about students as individuals and were concerned for their welfare. Hammond reported similar findings in middle years of high school. Although based on small research projects, these findings confirm earlier and more general research (Queensland School Reform Longitudinal Study, 2001) that found Australian schools generally are very strong in providing students with positive and inclusive learning environments. Overall, it appears that the nature of learning environments constitute a major strength in Australian schools.

While authors in the book acknowledge the significance of learning environments, we also argue that at-risk students need more. Coleman, for example, argues that 'pastoral' social support is insufficient to foster the academic success of at-risk students, and that by positioning students principally as recipients of pastoral care, teachers may unconsciously limit their access to the 'field of action' of academic achievement. Uptin's chapter provides evidence that students themselves resist such positioning. Her interviews with students show they do not want to be seen as 'different', nor do they want their backgrounds to be perceived as a 'problem'. Rather, they aim to be accepted as equals within their schools and within the wider Australian community.

Teaching and learning practices in focus

In various ways most chapters in the book address questions about the nature of current teaching and learning practices for at-risk EAL students in schools: the kinds of programs that are available to students; the extent to which they are provided with the support necessary to enable students to engage in mainstream programs; and the kind of support they receive for their academic language and literacy development. Coleman, Hammond and Miller and McCallum all report on research that found related patterns of strengths, and some limitations, in current teaching and learning practices.

Despite very positive learning environments at the level of whole school and individual classrooms, both Coleman's and Hammond's research identified areas of pedagogy that could be strengthened to better meet the needs of at-risk EAL students. In her research in primary schools, Coleman found that general expectations of at-risk students' academic abilities tended to be low, and that students were not sufficiently challenged or supported to engage in higher order thinking, or interpretation and transformation of knowledge. Hammond's research in middle years of high school identified somewhat similar patterns of classroom practices. She found that while high school students generally had more access to demanding curriculum content, they did not always receive enough of the kind of support that would enable them to engage at a deep level with that curriculum content, to engage in arguments and reasoning, to ask and explore questions, or to participate in discussions about curriculum concepts in a sustained way. Miller and McCallum point to similar findings in their chapter. They noted the dominance of teacher explanations in many classrooms and a lack of the kind of sequencing of small steps of interactive learning tasks and scaffolding necessary to support at-risk students in deep learning.

A number of factors appear to contribute to these patterns. Teachers in both Hammond's and Miller's research reported tensions resulting from competing needs on the one hand to meet compulsory curriculum requirements (that is, to 'get through the curriculum') and on the other to include more carefully sequenced and time-consuming tasks to support their at-risk EAL students. They also commented on the challenges of working with very diverse students within the one class who were at different educational levels and had very different educational, cultural, social and linguistic needs.

An additional factor was teachers' own limitations in knowledge of language and literacy Discussion of teachers' knowledge about language was a recurring theme across chapters, and authors reported similar findings from their research: that relatively few mainstream teachers had access to prior professional development in language and literacy education; that while most teachers were very aware that language and literacy development was the greatest area of need for their at-risk EAL students, many said they lacked the requisite knowledge and confidence to be able to support their students' language and literacy development within their classes. They were also unsure how to incorporate systematic and explicit teaching of academic language and literacy into across-the-curriculum programs. As noted in Chapter 1, Australian and international research has consistently highlighted concerns regarding teachers' own (lack of) knowledge about language in providing support for their students. The findings reported in chapters of this book are consistent with outcomes from previous research (Hammond, 2008; Jones

& Chen, 2012; Macken-Horarik, Love & Unsworth, 2011; Watkins, Lean, Noble & Dunn, 2013), and indicate the need for more professional support for teachers in the area of language and literacy education – support for teachers that would have positive implications for all students, but especially for at-risk EAL students.

This question of knowledge about language and literacy highlights the significance of the recently introduced Australian Curriculum. Of particular value is the English component of the Curriculum (ACARA, 2012) and the priority it places, through its strands of Language and Literacy on students' *use* of language and literacy, as well as *knowledge about* language and literacy. The detail it provides of whole text analysis; cohesion; sentence grammar; morphology; and spelling is of real value to teachers working with at-risk EAL students. Also of value is the accompanying EAL/D Teacher Resource document (ACARA, 2011). At this point in time, it is not clear how outcomes from the current review of the Australian Curriculum may impact on these documents. Despite this uncertainty, authors in the book see the documents as validating the importance of knowledge about language, and also as providing important resources for schools and teachers seeking ways of building in support for their at-risk EAL students' academic language and literacy development within the context of mainstream schooling. It is to be hoped that ongoing implementation of the Australian Curriculum will enhance teachers' knowledge and confidence, and assist them meet curriculum demands while also providing necessary high levels of support, especially with language and literacy development, for their At Risk EAL students.

In sum, the chapters of the book point to some consistent patterns in teaching and learning practices: they highlight important strengths in the nature of learning environments at school and classroom levels; but they also highlight a number of areas where teaching and learning practices could be reviewed and strengthened. These include:

- systematic planning of high-challenge programs to engage all students
- systematic connections between students' backgrounds and prior knowledge, including prior learning, and educational knowledge
- discussion of learning: including discussion of purposes of learning within units, lessons and specific tasks (that is, discussion of why it is important to learn specific educational concepts, and what is the significance of these concepts beyond school; how tasks and lessons contribute to that learning); and more reflection on what students have learned
- targeted scaffolding to ensure that small steps in learning are available to students
- systematic teaching of language and literacy across all curriculum subjects, including basic elements of literacy (phonology, spelling, vocabulary) to support low literacy students
- 'unpacking' of assessment tasks.

At issue here is not the capacity or willingness of individual teachers to address the needs of their at-risk EAL students. Rather, the findings raise questions about the demands faced by individual teachers who are balancing competing pressures and juggling needs of very diverse groups of students within their mainstream classes, and the extent to which school, and more generally, the educational system supports teachers in this task. A key priority here is reducing pressure to 'get through the curriculum' in order to enable space for a greater emphasis on deep knowledge and deep learning – and in the case of at-risk EAL students, the additional time that deep learning will require. Such an issue can only be addressed at system and school levels. However, the consistency of findings reported in the chapters suggest that education systems and schools could usefully focus professional support for teachers of at-risk EAL students around areas that have been listed earlier.

Ways forward

So how could these areas be addressed?

All chapters in the book in various ways have addressed implications for working with at-risk EAL students in mainstream schools. While Cranitch and Uptin focused primarily on who at-risk EAL students are, and what they bring to the task of learning at school, other chapters have addressed implications for the design and implementation of programs that meet the needs of at-risk EAL students. Chapters 6, 7 and 8 in particular, address ways forward in work with EAL students in mainstream classrooms. Across the chapters, there are a number of recurring issues:

- the significance of high-challenge programs and high teacher expectations
- the need for 'designed-in' and 'contingent' scaffolding (Hammond & Gibbons, 2005) that provides differential and targeted levels of support; and, most obviously
- systematic and explicit teaching of, and about, academic language and literacy.

Perhaps the most contentious aspect of the book is the argument that at-risk EAL students can and should engage with high-challenge programs. How realistic is it to expect students with substantial educational gaps and low levels of literacy to participate with their English-speaking peers in programs that are characterised by high intellectual challenge? And how can teachers provide the differential levels of support necessary for students with very different educational levels and abilities to engage with this intellectual challenge? What might all this look like in practice?

In their chapter, Miller and McCallum address such questions directly. They argue that, for at-risk EAL students at least initially, this may mean that learning activities need to be modified to ensure students are able to participate. It may also mean that written texts need to be modified in terms of grammatical structure and vocabulary to ensure they are comprehensible to the students. One of the contributions of this chapter is its model of literacy and proposals for working with low-level literacy students. A key argument in the book, however, is that such modifications need to be seen as temporary, and as providing a means to the end of enabling students to begin the process of educational 'catch-up'. As Dooley (in Chapter 7) argues, if students are to have equitable access to education, then programs need to be 'intellectually rigorous, pedagogically engaging and socioculturally supportive'.

The program outlined in Dooley's chapter provides insights into what such programs might look like. As with other students, at-risk EAL learners need an environment in which they are supported to work just beyond their current capabilities but within a *Zone of Proximal Development* (ZPD) (Vygotsky, 1978), that is, a space where they are able to complete learning activities at a level that is currently a little beyond them, but achievable with the teacher's support. The after-school MediaClub program described by Dooley captures this principle. Throughout the program, students worked towards a final task of producing a music track, recording it and burning it to CD. To enable them to achieve this task (beyond their initial capabilities), students were supported in the program to learn technical and operational skills for GarageBand software; to learn oral and written literacy required for their song; and to learn about audio meaning making. The program captured the students' passion for music and for singing, and positioned them as potential experts; it provided them with digitalised and targeted scaffolding to develop skills that were perceived by students as purposeful; and it supported students' language and literacy development through their engagement with skills and final task. As Dooley argues, the MediaClub program included features that complemented and extended formal school programs.

However, how can such features be incorporated successfully in formal school programs? What do they look like in the context of mainstream classes? In Chapter 8, Miller addresses such questions through her focus on ways of 'closing the gap' for at-risk EAL students. She stresses the importance of using language in context and of integrating an explicit language focus with the teaching of curriculum content. The strategies she provides can be incorporated into existing programs, but in ways that enable teachers to build in necessary levels of support and to 'amplify the curriculum' (Gibbons, 2014). As a final comment, the following examples are also offered to illustrate how some teachers have approached the design and implementation of high-challenge and high-support programs that are inclusive of all students, including at-risk EAL students. (These examples are drawn from previous research by Hammond & Gibbons, 2005 and Michell & Sharpe, 2005, and from professional development programs undertaken in collaboration with NSW Department of Education and Communities.)

Example 1: The Sunrise show

In a Year 4 HSIE program, students studied a unit of work on the Antarctic. A major component of the program was the culminating task of preparing for and presenting a 'Sunrise Show' about the Antarctic. This task was modelled on a current Australian morning television show: it was 'hosted' by two students, and involved presentations from other groups of students on segments about weather patterns, specific animals or birds, survival strategies and so on. An audience consisting of students from other classes and families were invited to attend the final presentation of the 'show' at the end of the program. In designing the unit, the teacher selected and sequenced tasks to enable students to build the necessary skills and knowledge to complete the culminating task of planning and presenting the Sunrise show.

Example 2: The Magazine project

As part of a program that aimed to support middle year refugee background students a teacher and students negotiated the major task that would form the core of their program. They decided on 'the Magazine Project' – a project that involved the development of a 'teen girl' magazine that aimed to provide new students with the kind of information that would help them adjust to school in Australia and life in the local community. The magazine was 'launched' with a video made by the students, and speeches by the students to an invited audience from the school and broader community. In designing the program, the teacher identified relevant skills that students would need to produce the Magazine and she planned sequential lessons around development of these skills, and around teaching the relevant aspects of language and literacy

A number of features, common to the two examples above, were also highlighted across the chapters of the book as especially relevant to the education of at-risk EAL students.

1 Like the MediaClub program described by Dooley, both programs were planned around completion of a culminating high-challenge task, or 'Rich Task' (New Basics Project, 2001). Such tasks have a high level of intellectual challenge. They are perceived by both teacher and students as being of educational value and interest, and as having a significance beyond the classroom. As a result, both teacher and students in the two examples were prepared to put in the necessary time and effort to work towards completion of the task.

2 In both programs the culminating Rich Task was 'designed-in' (Hammond & Gibbons, 2005) as part of the process of program planning. That is, the design of the task took account of the curriculum goals, and the students' existing knowledge and abilities. It also provided the basis for backward mapping (Wiggins & McTighe, 2005) whereby the teachers planned backwards from the specific demands of the final task to identify the various skills (including aspects of language and literacy) students would need to complete the task. Teachers then selected and sequenced classroom activities to build those necessary skills. In both programs, there was extensive skill development, however teacher and students perceived these skills as a means to a purposeful end, rather than an end in themselves.

3 The process of backward mapping from the Rich Task provided the context for ongoing discussions between teacher and students of purposes of learning: of what students needed to learn and why in relation to the program as a whole, to specific lessons, and to individual learning tasks. As a result students could see a legitimate reason for engaging in specific learning tasks and of learning skills. Students were also encouraged to think about and discuss their own learning (of particular relevance to at-risk students who were unfamiliar with some of the teaching and learning practices they encountered in these programs, and with some school expectations of student behaviour).

The design of both programs provided the context for high levels of differential support. In order to complete the various sub-tasks and build towards completion of the Rich Task, students participated in activities that shifted between whole class, group and individual work. Whole-class activities ensured all students worked towards the common goal of completing the Rich Task; however groups of students worked on different sub-components of the task. As a result, the teacher was able to build in high levels of scaffolding in response to the different abilities and needs of students within each group. Where necessary, sub-tasks were sequenced to ensure there were small steps in learning so students could successfully engage with them.

4 Both programs included extensive and focused teaching of language and literacy. The design of the programs, with culminating Rich Task and contributing sub-tasks,

provided the context for analysis of students' language and literacy needs and analysis of curriculum demands. Thus teaching of relevant aspects of language and literacy was 'designed-in' to support students in their work towards completion of sub-tasks and final Rich Task. Such language and literacy teaching was seen as purposeful and as integrated with the teaching of curriculum content. In addition, because different groups worked on different sub-tasks, additional support could be provided for specific students as necessary.

5 Both programs provided students with access to high levels of message abundancy (Gibbons, 2003; 2009a). As Hammond reported, in Chapter 5, the notion of 'message abundancy' arose again and again in her interviews with teachers and with students about what helped students most in their schoolwork. The sequencing of tasks provided opportunities for students to visit and revisit the same concepts again and again – through oral discussions; through group interactions; through library research; through analysis of models of oral (the Sunrise program) or written texts (the magazine project); through guided support in writing specific texts; and through opportunities to interact with multimodal texts.

6 Teachers' expectations of what students could and should achieve were high, but realistic. The design of the Rich Tasks aimed for high standards of educational achievement, but nature of the designed-in and contingent support ensured students were able to develop the necessary skills, including language and literacy skills to achieve those high educational standards.

The task of designing and implementing programs in mainstream classes where at-risk EAL students are both challenged and supported is not easy. Nor is the task of integrating the teaching of language and literacy across the curriculum in ways that effectively address the diverse needs of students. The chapters in this book provide some insights into ways of meeting this challenge. Hopefully, these insights may be of use to all those who are concerned with the education of at-risk EAL students, especially those who are mainstream teachers.

Glossary

academic literacy – knowledge of how academic texts are structured: generic transferable skills for reading, writing, and presenting school texts and for successfully engaging with academic tasks

BICS* – Basic Interpersonal Communication Skills (language used in day-to-day procedural and social interactions, eg buying bus ticket; speaking with a friend)

CALP* – Cognitive Academic Language Proficiency (written or spoken language needed to engage with academic tasks at school) – this is not acquired 'naturally' in interaction and requires explicit teaching

comprehensible input – a term originally introduced by Stephen Krashen in the 1970s to refer to explanations or texts that are only slightly more difficult than those which students can already understand; he called this *i+1*, meaning input + a bit of additional challenge

comprehensible output – a term introduced by Merrill Swain in 1985 which is now taken to refer to opportunities for students to practise language at their level of competency – this can be written or spoken

content-based literacy – teaching literacy and language through subject matter such as Science, Maths, Social Science or other texts

critical reading – reading beyond literal meanings to include evaluation of information, causes, implications and inference

EAL – English as an Additional Language: the preferred term in all Australian states to describe learners of second or subsequent languages; alternative term used elsewhere is ESL (English as a Second Language)

essential questions – questions that stimulate thinking, inquiry and understanding of core curriculum elements; Examples could include: *Why are scientists concerned with cause and effect? Why do societies have laws?*

evidence-based pedagogy – teaching based on principles and outcomes shown in research

genres – written or spoken text types, eg. narrative, recount, persuasive text, different types of poetry, cartoons.

high frequency words – words often used in everyday language, or in certain academic texts. There are many online lists of high frequency words for different learning levels

higher order thinking skills (HOTS) – a concept related to the upper levels of Bloom's taxonomy, this is the learning of complex critical skills such as analysis, evaluation, or application – HOTS assume a baseline level of comprehension

L1 – first language or mother tongue; it contrasts with **L2** (second language)

language recycling – systematic reuse of taught language structures and vocabulary to promote acquisition and learning

language field – vocabulary and language structures associated with a particular topic

lexis – vocabulary

lexical density – degree or amount of challenging vocabulary within a text; typically lexical density is higher in written than spoken texts and because lexical density is often very high in written academic texts, many students find such texts difficult to read

literate talk – use of oral language to discuss academic concepts – such talk reflects the more complex vocabulary and structures of written texts, and provides a bridge between everyday oral language and academic literacy

* term introduced in 1979 by Canadian language development researcher Professor Jim Cummins

mainstream text – text written for native speakers with age appropriate schooling

message abundancy – a term introduced by Pauline Gibbons, referring to multiple variations of similar messages or concepts – for example, repetition of words or phrases, paraphrase, visual demonstration of a concept, hands-on engagement, oral discussion, diagrammatic support, word lists of key vocabulary

metacognitive strategies – strategies that focus on thinking as part of learning, such as planning (brainstorm, diagram, concept map); self-checking; think-alouds, or use of mnemonics for memory; reflection on what has been learned – metacognitive strategies require explicit teaching

metalanguage – language used to discuss, describe or analyse language, eg, all grammatical terms, text organisation, choice of vocabulary.

modelling – providing an example of a specific text type (genre), or giving a clear, worked-through example of a task, demonstrating how to complete a task

morphology – patterns of word formation, including prefixes, suffixes, all endings for a word, eg, *repeat, repeating, repetition, repeatedly*

multimodal texts – a combination of words, diagrams, video, images, or graphics within text – websites and picture books are multimodal.

passive voice – non-active verb form, eg, *The water was placed in a beaker.* contrasts with 'active voice' version – *I placed the water in the beaker.*

redundancy – repetition of vocabulary, concepts or structures within a text

register – language used for a specific purpose in a specific social context – registers may be formal or informal and vary with topic, relationship between speakers or writers and mode (spoken, written, multimodal)

Rich Task – a culminating task with significant intellectual challenge that draws together understandings and skills developed across a program – Rich Tasks in primary schools might include: English – interview a resident of a nursing home and write his/her biography; Science – prepare and present a multimedia talk on a specific disease of the human body

scaffolding – specific support given to students that pushes them to work just beyond their current capabilities; 'designed-in' or macro level scaffolding refers to program planning that builds in opportunities for targeted support; contingent, or micro-level scaffolding refers to the support that is provided to students at the point of need and as lessons unfold

syntax – word order or sequence in which words are put together to form sentences – syntax differs greatly between languages

syntactic complexity – amount and degree of complex sentences within a text

Note to teachers

Any of these terms can be searched online for additional explanations, including detailed definitions, explanations of theoretical underpinnings, related research articles, educational applications, and original sources.

References

ACARA, 2009, 'The Shape of the Australian Curriculum' Version 2.0, viewed 3 January 2015, <http://www.acara.edu.au/verve/_resources/the_shape_of_the_australian_curriculum_v4.pdf>.

ACARA, 2011, 'English as an Additional Language or Dialect: Teacher Resource', Version 1.2, viewed 3 January 2015, http://www.acara.edu.au/verve/_resources/the_shape_of_the_australian_curriculum_v4.pdf>.

ACARA, 2012, 'The Australian Curriculum, English', Version 3.0, viewed 3 January 2015, <http://www.australiancurriculum.edu.au/english/curriculum/f-10>.

ACARA 2013, 'English as an Additional Language or Dialect Teacher Resource' *(May, 2014 Version)* viewed 11 November 2014 <http://www.acara.edu.au>.

ACARA 2015, English overview, viewed 19 January 2015, viewed 3 January 2015 <http://www.australiancurriculum.edu.au/english/content-structure/literacy>.

Ausubel, DP 1968, *Educational psychology: A cognitive view*, Holt Rinehart and Winston Inc., New York.

Australian Bureau of Statistics 2013, *Quick stats*, viewed 17 October 2014, <http://www.censusdata.abs.gov.au/census_services/getproduct/census/2011/quickstat/ >.

Australian Institute for Teaching and School Leadership (AITSL) 2011, 'National Professional Standards for Teachers', viewed 20 November, 2014, <http://www.aitsl.edu.au>.

Brown, J, Miller, J & Mitchell, J 2006, 'Interrupted schooling and the acquisition of literacy: Experiences of Sudanese refugees in Victorian secondary schools', *Australian Journal of Language and Literacy*, 29(2), 150–162.

Brown, G & Brown, S 2012, 'Education in Burma: Guaranteeing hope for a better future', viewed 4 June 2014 < http://gordonandsarahbrown.com/wp-content/uploads/2012/06/Note-on-Education-in-Burma.pdf>.

Burgoyne, U & Hull, O 2007, 'Good practice guide: Teaching learners from highly oral cultures', National Centre for Vocational Education Research, viewed 20 January 2015, <http://trove.nla.gov.au/version/43649901>.

Burma Link, 2013, 'Background: refugee camps', viewed 4 June 2014 <http://www.burmalink.org/background/thailand-burma-border/displaced-in-thailand/refugee-camps/>.

Carrasquillo, A & London, C 1993, *Parents and schools*, Garland Publishing, New York.

Christie, F 2002, *Classroom discourse analysis. A functional perspective*, Continuum, London

Christie, F 2005, *Language education in the primary years*, UNSW Press, Sydney.

Christie, P & Sidhu, R 2002, 'Responding to globalisation: Refugees and the challenges facing Australian schools', viewed 10 May 2011, <http://www.arts.uwa.edu.au/MotsPluriels/MP2102pcrs.html. >.

Coady, M, Hamann, ET, Harrington, M, Pho, S & Yedlin, J 2008, 'Successful schooling for ELLs: Principles for building responsive learning environments', in LS Verplaetse & N Migliacci (eds), *Inclusive pedagogy for English language learners: A handbook of research-informed practices*, Lawrence Erlbaum Associates, New York & London.

Cassity, E & Gow, G 2006, 'Shifting space and cultural place: The transition experiences of African young people in western Sydney high schools', Paper presented at the AARE International Education Research Conference.

Coleman, J 2012, 'The ESL teacher as "productive" pedagogical mentor', *TESOL in Context, Special Edition S3*, viewed 4 December 2014, <http://www.tesol.org.au/Publications/Special-Editions>.

Collier, V & Thomas, W 2009, *Educating English learners for a transformed world,* Fuente Press, Albuquerque, NM.

Commonwealth of Australia 2006, 'Congolese Community Profile', viewed 22 January 2015 <http://www.scoa.org.au/resources/277479_72752_community-profile-congo.pdf >.

Cranitch, M 2010, 'Developing language and Literacy skills to support refugee students in the transition from primary to secondary school', *Australian Journal of Language and Literacy,* 33 (3), 255–267.

Cranitch, M & Macfarlane, T 2011, 'Jesuit Refugee Service: Evaluation Report', (unpublished report).

Cummins, J 1981, 'The role of primary language development in promoting educational success for language minority students', in *Schooling and language minority students: A theoretical framework* California State Department of Education, Sacramento, pp. 3–49.

Cummins, J 2000, *Language, power and pedagogy: Bilingual children in the crossfire*, Multilingual Matters, Clevedon, UK.

Cummins, J 2001, 'Magic Bullets and the Grade 4 slump: Solutions from technology', *NABE News, 25*(1), 4-6.

Cummins, J 2008, 'BICS and CALP: Empirical and theoretical status of the distinction', in B Street & NH Hornberger (eds), *Encyclopedia of language and education, Volume 2: Literacy,* 2nd edn, Springer Science + Business Media LLC, New York, pp. 71–83.

Cummins, J & Early, M 2011, *Identity texts: The collaborative creation of power in multilingual schools,* Trentham Books, Stoke on Trent, UK.

Darling-Hammond, L & Schon, E 1996, 'Who teaches and why: Dilemmas for building a profession for twenty-first century schools', in J Sikula, T Buttery & E Guyton (eds), *Handbook of research on teacher education*, Macmillan, New York, pp. 67–101.

Davis-Warra, J, Dooley, K, & Exley, B 2011, 'Reflecting on the Dream Circle : Urban Indigenous education processes designed for student and community empowerment', *QTU Professional Magazine, 26,* pp. 19–21. http://eprints.qut.edu.au/48447/.

Department of Education and Early Childhood Development (DEECD) 2008, 'Strengthening outcomes: Refugee students in government schools', Department of Education and Early Childhood Development Melbourne, Victoria.

Department of Immigration and Border Protection, Canberra, 2013, 'Australia's Refugee and Humanitarian Program', Fact Sheet 60, viewed 20 October, 2014, <http://www.immi.gov.au/media/fact-sheets>.

Dooley, K 2009, 'Re-thinking pedagogy for middle school students, with little, no or severely interrupted schooling', *English Teaching: Practice and critique*, 8(1), 5–22.

Earnest, J, Housen, T & Gillieatt, S 2007, 'A new cohort of refugee students in Perth: Challenges for students and educators', in *Student Engagement*, Proceedings of the 16th Annual Teaching and Learning Forum, 30-31 Jan 2007, Perth: The University of Western Australia, viewed 3 January 2015, <http://lsn.curtin.edu.au/tlf.tlf2007/refereed/earnest.html.>

Education Queensland 2002, *A Guide to productive pedagogies, classroom reflection manual,* Teaching and Learning Branch, Curriculum Implementation Unit, Brisbane.

Foucault, M 1983, 'The subject and power', in H Dreyfus & P Rainbow, (eds), *Michel Foucault: Beyond structuralism and Hermeneutics*, University of Chicago, Chicago, pp. 208–226.

Freeman, Y & Freeman, D 2007, 'Four keys for school success for Elementary English Learners', in J Cummins & C Davison (eds), *International handbook of English Language Teaching*, Springer, Norwell, MA

Gibbons, P 1991, *Learning to learn in a second language*, PETAA, Sydney.

Gibbons, P 2002, *Scaffolding language, scaffolding learning: Teaching ESL children in the mainstream classroom*, Heinemann, Portsmouth, NH.

Gibbons, P 2003, 'Mediating language learning: Teacher interactions with ESL students in a content-based classroom', *TESOL Quarterly*, 37(2), 247–273.

Gibbons, P 2008, '"It was taught good and I learned a lot": Intellectual practices and ESL learners in the middle years', *Australian Journal of Language and Literacy*, 31 (2), 155–173.

Gibbons, P 2009a, *Challenging expectations: Literacy, intellectual quality and English language learners in the middle years*, Heinemann, Portsmouth, NH.

Gibbons, P 2009b, *English learners, academic literacy and thinking. Learning in the challenge zone,* Heinemann, Portsmouth NH.

Gibbons, P (2014) *Scaffolding language, scaffolding learners: Teaching English language learners in the mainstream classroom*, (2nd edn), Heinemann, Portsmouth NH.

Gifford, SM, Correa-Velez, I & Sampson, R 2009, 'Good starts for recently arrived youth with refugee backgrounds: Promoting wellbeing in the first three years of settlement in Melbourne', viewed 3 January 2015, http://www.myan.org.au/file/file/useful%20 resources/report-good-starts.pdf

Gonzalez, JE & Darling-Hammond, L 2000, *Programs that prepare teachers to work effectively with students learning English*, Eric Digest [Electronic Version], viewed 21 January 2015, <http://eric.ed.gov/?q=Programs+that+prepare+teachers+to+work+effectively+with+students+learning+English%2c&id=ED447724>.

Government of Western Australia 2012, 'New and emerging communities in Western Australia', viewed 31 October, 2014, <http://www.omi.wa.gov.au/resources/publications/community_profiles/New_and_Emerging_Communities.pd >.

Hammond, J 2001, 'Scaffolding and language', in J. Hammond (ed.), *Scaffolding: Teaching and learning in language and literacy education*, PETAA, Sydney, pp. 15–30.

Hammond, J 2008, 'Intellectual challenge and ESL students: Implications of quality teaching initiatives', Special Focus Issue, *Australian Journal of Language and Literacy*, 31(2), 128–154.

Hammond, J 2009, 'High challenge, high support programmes with English as a second language learners: A teacher-researcher collaboration', in J Miller, A Kostogriz & M Gearon (eds), *Culturally and linguistically diverse classrooms: New dilemmas for teachers,* Multilingual Matters, Bristol, pp. 56–74.

Hammond, J 2012, 'Hope and challenge in the Australian Curriculum: Implications for EAL students and their teachers', *Australian Journal of Language and Literacy*, 35(2), 223–240.

Hammond, J 2014a, 'The transition of refugee students from Intensive English Centres to mainstream high schools: Current practices and future possibilities', Final Report, NSW Department of Education and Communities.

Hammond, J 2014b, 'An Australian perspective on standards-based education, teacher knowledge and English as an Additional Language students, *TESOL Quarterly*, 48(3), 507–532.

Hammond J & Gibbons, P 2005, 'Putting scaffolding to work: The contribution of scaffolding in articulating ESL education', *Prospect*, 20(1), 6–30.

Hammond J & M Macken-Horarik 2001, 'Teachers' voices, teachers' practices: Insider perspectives on literacy education', *Australian Journal of Language and Literacy*, 24(2), 112–132.

Hattam, R & Every, D 2010, 'Teaching in fractured classrooms: Refugee education, public culture, community and ethics', *Race Ethnicity and Education*, 13(4), 409–424.

Hattie, J 2009, *Visible learning – A synthesis of over 800 meta-analyses relating to achievement*, Routledge, Abingdon, UK.

Haywood, L, Hajdukowski-Ahmed, M, Ploeg, J & Trollope-Kumar, K 2008, '"We want to talk they give us pills": Identity and mental health of refugee women from Sudan', in M Hajdukowski-Ahmed, N Khanlou, & H Moussa, , (eds) *Not born a refugee: Woman contesting identities, rethinking practices*, Studies in Forced Migration, Volume 24, Berghahn Books, New York & Oxford.

Hutchinson, M & Dorsett, P 2012, 'What does the literature say about refugee people? Implications for practice', *Journal of Social Inclusion*. 3(2) 55–78.

Ito, M, Baumer, S, Bittanti, M, Boyd, D, Cody, R, Herr-Stephenson, B, Horst, HA, Lange, PG, Mahendran, D, Martínez, KZ and 5 other colleagues 2010, *Hanging out, messing around, and geeking out*, The MIT Press, Cambridge, MA.

Jones, P & Chen, H 2012, 'Teachers' knowledge about language: Issues of pedagogy and expertise', *Australian Journal of Language and Literacy*, 35(2), 14 –168.

Keddie, A 2011, 'Pursuing justice for refugee students: Addressing issues of cultural (mis)recognition', *International Journal of Inclusive Education*, 15(1), pp. 1–16.

Konu, AI, & Rimpela, MK 2002, 'Well-being in schools: A conceptual model', *Health Promotion International, 17*(1), 79–87.

Luke, A & Freebody, P 1999, 'A map of possible practices: Further notes on the four resources model', *Practically Primary*, *4*(2), 5–8.

Luke, A, Woods, A & Dooley, K 2011, 'Comprehension as social and intellectual practice: Rebuilding curriculum in low socioeconomic and cultural minority schools', *Theory into Practice, 50*, 2, 157–64.

Lustig SL, Kia-Keating, M, Knight, WG, Geltman, P, Ellis, H, Kinzie, JD, Keane, T & Saxe, GN 2004, 'Review of child and adolescent refugee mental health', *Journal of the American Academy of Child and Adolescent Psychiatry*, 43(1), 24–44.

MacBeth, J, Kirwan, T, Myers, K, McCall, J, Smith, I, McKay, E, Sharp, C, Bhabra, S, Weindling, D & Pocklington, K 2001, *The impact of study support: A report of a longitudinal study into the impact of participation in out-of-school hours learning on the academic attainment, attitudes and school attendance of secondary school students.* Research Report RR273, Colegate, Norwich: Department for Education and Skills, viewed 1 September 2014, < http://dera.ioe.ac.uk/4624/1/RR273.pdf >.

Macken-Horarik, M, Love K & Unsworth, L 2011, 'Grammatics good enough for school English in the 21st Century', *Australian Journal of Language and Literacy*, 34 (1), 9–23.

Matthews, J 2008, 'Schooling and settlement: Refugee education in Australia', *International Studies in Sociology of Education*, 23(56), 31–47.

Maybin, J, Mercer, N & Steirer, B 1992, 'Scaffolding learning in the classroom', in K Norman (ed.) *Thinking voices: The work of the National Oracy Project,* Hodder & Stoughton, Sevenoaks, Kent, pp. 186–195.

McCallum, M & Miller J 2013a, 'Supporting English as an additional language students in Science: integrating content and language', *Teaching Science, 59(2), 37–42.*

McCallum, M & Miller J 2013b, 'Science and language ecosystems unit for EAL students', viewed 19 January, 2015, <http://www.globaleducationresources.wikispaces.com >.

Michell, M. & Sharpe, T 2005, 'Collective instructional scaffolding in English as a Second Language classrooms', *Prospect*, 20 (1), 31–58.

Miller, JM, 2003, *Audible difference: ESL and social identity in schools,* Multilingual Matters, Clevedon, UK.

Miller, J 2009, 'Teaching refugee learners with interrupted education in science: Vocabulary, literacy and pedagogy, *International Journal of Science Education*, 31 (4), 571–592.

Miller, J 2013, 'Communicative content pedagogy: engaging students in reading comprehension', *English in Australia*, 48 (1), 36–45.

Miller J & Windle, J 2010, 'Second language literacy: Putting high needs ESL Learners in the frame', *English in Australia*, 45 (3), 31–40.

Miller, J, Mitchell, J & Brown, J 2005, 'African refugees with interrupted schooling in the high school mainstream: Dilemmas for teachers', *Prospect*, 20 (2), 19–33.

Miller, J, Keary, A & Windle, J 2012, 'Assessing the reading and writing of low literacy ESL students. *TESOL in Context*, Special Edition S3: November 2012, Ethics, Equity and Ecology.

Miller, J, Windle, J & Yazdanpanah, 2014, 'Planning lessons for refugee-background students: Challenges and strategies', *International Journal of Pedagogies and Learning,* Vol. 9 (1).

Mills, KA & Levido, A2011, 'iPed: Pedagogy for digital text production', *The Reading Teacher, 65,* 1, 80–91.

Morgan, AM, Comber, B, Freebody, P & Nixon, H 2014, *Literacy in the middle years: Learning from collaborative classroom research,* PETAA, Sydney.

Munns, G, Sawyer, W & Cole, B 2013, *Exemplary teachers of students in poverty*, Routledge, Oxon & New York.
Nation, P 2002, *Managing vocabulary learning*, SEAMEO Regional Language Centre, Singapore.
National Council of Teachers of English 2013, 'Formative assessment that truly informs instruction', viewed 14 October 2014, <http://www.ncte.org >.
Ndhlovu, F 2013, 'Language nesting, superdiversity and African diasporas in regional Australia', *Australian Journal of Linguistics, 33*, 4, 426–48.
Newby, L 2012, 'INEE: The Education Cluster thematic case study series', viewed 30 May 2014, < http://toolkit.ineesite.org/toolkit/INEEcms/uploads/1115/Education%20Cluster%20Thematic%20Case%20Studies%202012.pdf>.
Newmann, FM, Marks, H & Gamoran, A 1996, 'Authentic pedagogy and student performance', *American Journal of Education*, 104, 280–312.
Newmann, FM, & Associates 1996, *Authentic achievement: Restructuring schools for intellectual achievement*, Jossey-Bass, San Francisco.
New South Wales Department of Education and Training 2003, *Quality teaching in New South Wales public schools: Continuing discussion about classroom practices: Lesson Extracts K-10,* State of New South Wales, Sydney.
New South Wales Department of Education and Training 2006, *Quality Teaching in New South Wales Public Schools. A classroom practice guide,* New South Wales Department of Education and Training, Sydney.
Nieto, S & Bode, P 2008, *Affirming diversity,* 5th edn, Pearson, Boston, MA.
O'Neill, S & Gish, A 2008, *Teaching English as a second language*, Oxford University Press, Australia.
Quality Teaching in NSW Public schools: Discussion paper 2003, Professional Support and Curriculum Directorate, NSW DET.
Quality Teaching in NSW Public Schools: An assessment practice guide 2004, Professional Learning Directorate, NSW DET.
Queensland School Reform Longitudinal Study 2001, *Final Report*, Education Queensland, Brisbane.
Ramirez, M & Matthews, J 2008, 'Living in the NOW: Young people from refugee backgrounds pursuing respect, risk and fun', *Journal of Youth Studies*, 11(1), 83–92.
Save the Children Australia 2014, 'Personal Stories from Syrian children and families', viewed 30 May 2014, <http://www.scaemergency.org.au/personal-stories-from-syrian-children-and-families/
Schleppegrell, MJ 2007, 'The Linguistic challenges of mathematics teaching and learning: A research review, *Reading and Writing Quarterly*, 23: 139–159
Sharpe, T 2001, 'Scaffolding in action: Snapshots from the classroom', in J. Hammond (ed.), *Scaffolding: Teaching and learning in language and literacy education,* PETAA, Sydney, pp. 31–48.
Simpson, A & Walsh, M 2014, 'Pedagogic conceptualisations for touch pad technologies', *Australian Journal of Language and Literacy, 37,* 2, 128–38.
Sinclair, J & Coulthard, R 1975, *Towards an analysis of discourse: The English used by teachers and pupils*, Oxford University Press, London.
Smith, M (ed), 2004, 'Warehousing refugees: A denial of rights, a waste of humanity', viewed 2 June 2014, <http://www.uscrirefugees.org/2010Website/5_Resources/5_5_Refugee_Warehousing/5_5_3_Translations/Warehousing_Refugees_A_Denial_of_Rights.pdf>.
Steer, N 2014, 'Stories from the Field', UNHCR, viewed 30 May 2014, <http://www.unrefugees.org.au/our-stories/stories-from-the-field/naomi-steer,-australia-for-unhcr>.
Stern. J 2013, 'Life as one of the most persecuted ethnic groups on the planet', *The Atlantic,* 21 May 2013, viewed 30 May 2014, <http://www.theatlantic.com/international/archive/2013/05/life-as-one-of-the-most-persecuted-ethnic-groups-on-the-planet/276060/>.
Swain, M 2000, 'The output hypothesis and beyond: Mediating acquisition through collaborative dialogue', in J Lantolf (ed.), *Sociocultural theory and second language learning,* Oxford University Press, Oxford, pp. 97–114.
The New Basics Project 2001, *New Basics: The why, what, how and when of Rick Tasks*, Education Queensland, Brisbane.
Thomas, WP & Collier, VP 1997, *School effectiveness for language minority students,* The National Clearinghouse for Bilingual Education, George Washington University, Washington DC.
Tran, M 2013, 'Global development: Syrian refugees put strain on Jordan Schools amid fears for "lost generation"', *The Guardian,* 3 December 2013, viewed 2 June 2014,
<http://www.theguardian.com/global-development/2013/dec/02/syrian-refugees-strain-on-jordan-schools>.
UNHCR 17–23 May 2014, 'Inter-agency regional response for Syrian refugees: Egypt, Iraq, Jordan, Lebanon, Turkey', viewed 2 June 2014, < http://data.unhcr.org/syrianrefugees/regional.php#>.
UNHCR June, 2014, 'World Refugee Day: Global forced displacement tops 50 million for first time in post-World War II era', viewed 25 June 2014, <http://www.unhcr.org/53a155bc6.html>.
UNICEF March 2013, 'Supply and logistics: School in a box', viewed 25 June 2014, <http://www.unicef.org/supply/index_40377.html>.
UNICEF 2013, 'Shattered lives: Challenges and priorities for Syrian children and women in Jordan', viewed June 26 2014, < http://www.unicef.org/infobycountry/files/Shattered_Lives_June10.pdf>.

Uptin, J, Wright, J & Harwood, V 2013, '"It felt like I was a black dot on white paper": Examining young former refugees' experience of entering Australian high schools', *Australian Educational Researcher* 40, 125–137.

van Lier, L 1996, *Interaction in the language curriculum: Awareness, autonomy and authenticity,* Longman, London.

Valdes, G 2001, *Learning and not learning English: Latino students in American schools,* Teachers College Press, New York.

Vickers, M 2007, 'Developing university-community partnerships to support African refugees in greater Western Sydney', *Australian Journal of University Community Engagement*, 2 (1), 211–217.

Vygotsky, L 1978, *Mind in society: The development of higher psychological processes*, eds, M Cole, V John-Steiner, S Scribner & E Souberman, Harvard University Press, Cambridge MA.

Wagner, R, Muse, A & Tannenbaum, K 2007, *Vocabulary acquisition: Implications for reading comprehension,* Guildford Press, UK.

Walker, A, Shafer, J & Liams, M 2004, '"Not in my classroom": Teacher attitudes towards english language learners in the mainstream classroom', *NABE Journal of Research and Practice, 2*(1), 130–160.

Walqui, A 2006, 'Scaffolding instruction for English language learners: A conceptual framework', *International Journal of Bilingual Education and Bilingualism, 9* (2), 159–180.

Walsh, M, Cranitch, M, & Maras, K 2012, 'Into the deep end: the experience with *Flotsam* in Australia', *TESOL in Context* Special Edition S3, 1-16.

Waters, T & LeBlanc, K 2005, 'Refugees and education: Mass public schooling without a nation-state', *Comparative Education Review*. 49: 2.

Watkins, M, Lean, G, Noble, G, & Dunn, K 2013, 'Rethinking multiculturalism, reassessing multicultural education, Project Report Number 1 surveying New South Wales Public School Teachers', University of Western Sydney, Department of Education and Communities, and NSW Institute of Teachers.

Wedin, A 2010, 'A restricted curriculum for second language learners-a self-fulfilling teacher strategy?', *Language and Education, 24* (3), 171–183.

Wiggins, G & McTighe, J 2005, *Understanding by Design* (expanded 2nd edn), Association for Supervision and Curriculum Development (ASCD), Alexandria, VA.

Windle J & Miller J 2012, 'Approaches to teaching low literacy refugee-background students', *Australian Journal of Language and Literacy*. 35 (3) 317–333.

Woods, A, Levido, A, Dezuanni, M & Dooley, K 2014. Running a MediaClub – What's involved? And why would you bother? *Literacy Learning: The Middle Years*, *33* (3), 18-23.

Woods, A, Dooley, K, Luke, A & Exley, B 2014, 'School leadership, literacy and social justice: The place of local school curriculum planning and reform', in I Bogotch & C Shields (eds), *The International Handbook on Social[In]Justice and Educational Leadership,* Springer, New York, pp. 509–20.

Wynn, J 2007, 'Learning to become somebody well: Challenges for educational policy', Australian Educational Researcher, 34(3), 35–52.

Yang, L & Wilson, K 2006, 'Second language classroom reading: A social constructivist approach', *The Reading Matrix*, 6 (3), 364–372.

Useful websites for teachers

ACARA English as an additional language or dialect: teacher resources. EAL/D Learning progression document as well as annotated content descriptions for various curriculum areas from Foundation to Year 10.

http://www.acara.edu.au/curriculum/student_diversity/eald_teacher_resource.html

Australian Government Department of Immigration and Border Protection Government policies about immigration, visa classes and Australian citizenship.

http://www.immi.gov.au/

Breaking News English This website focuses on current news and includes teaching plans for issues that are present in today's media. Each plan includes warm-up activities, pre-reading or pre-listening activities, discussion questions, writing activities, and language focus activities. It is British-based but four different levels for tasks and many interesting texts and videos for children.

http://www.breakingnewsenglish.com/

Centre for Multicultural Youth Homepage On-line resources for teachers as well as useful links to other agencies.

http://www.cmy.net.au/

Foundation House: Victorian Foundation for Survivors of Torture Counselling services in Victoria. Child adolescent and family program. Useful on-line resources for schools. http://www.foundationhouse.org.au/ (homepage)

http://www.foundationhouse.org.au/resources/ (resources page)

Count me in Government of South Australia Department of Education and Children's Services

A resource to support ESL students with refugee experience in schools. http://www.decd.sa.gov.au/literacy/files/links/Count_me_in.pdf

Kids Matter: Australian Primary Schools Mental Health Initiative Rainbow program for children in refugee families run in conjunction with Foundation House Victoria with programs throughout Australia.

https://www.kidsmatter.edu.au/primary/programs/rainbow-program-children-refugee-families

Multicultural Youth Advocacy Network A national advisory and advocacy network on multicultural youth issues – produces resources and reports

http://www.myan.org.au

Roads to Refuge NSW Department of Education and Communities: Factual information about asylum seekers and refugees, teaching ideas and videos about refugee issues. This website provides resources for raising awareness about refugee students (rather than how to teach them).

http://www.roads-to-refuge.com.au/index.html

The film clips on this page provide details of what schools are doing to support refugee students:

http://www.roads-to-refuge.com.au/refugees-australia/supporting-education.html

NSW Refugee Health Service Resources and fact sheets for schools working with refugee students and families (health and nutrition)

http://www.swslhd.nsw.gov.au/refugee/

Refugee Handbook for Schools New Zealand Ministry of Education English for Speakers of other languages: Useful information about whole school policy and practices.

http://www.minedu.govt.nz/NZEducation/EducationPolicies/Schools/EnglishForSpeakersOfOtherLanguages/MaterialsResources/ESOLRefugeeHandbook.aspx

Supporting English Language Learners with limited prior schooling A practical guide for educators. Ontario Ministry of Education

http://www.edu.gov.on.ca/eng/document/manyroots/schooling.html

Queensland Program of Assistance to Survivors of Torture & Trauma Inc. (QPASTT) A teachers' guide to working with students from refugee and displaced persons background.

http://qpastt.org.au/tbcwp1/wp-content/uploads/2014/05/School-teachers-guide-2007-updated-2104.pdf

Racism no way Anti-racism education for Australian schools with teacher resources, information sheets about different communities.

http://www.racismnoway.com.au/index.html

Reading Australia Educational resources on Australian books for all reading levels – online resources are for teachers and students.

http://readingaustralia.com.au/

Refugee Council of Australia Peak advocacy body with up-to-date information about Australian government policies about asylum seekers and refugees with links to other relevant agencies. http://www.refugeecouncil.org.au/ (homepage)

http://www.refugeecouncil.org.au/resources/for-teachers/ (resources for teachers)

STARTTS NSW Service for the Treatment and Rehabilitation of Torture and Trauma Survivors.
Counselling services in NSW– Psychevisual online Lectures provide useful training for professionals working with people from a refugee background.

http://www.startts.org.au

Student Handouts and educational materials This site provides a range of free printable graphic organiser worksheets. You are able to manipulate these to suit lesson objectives.

http://www.studenthandouts.com/graphicorganizers.htm

Teaching Refugees Primarily a Canadian website, but provides useful strategies and resources for teachers teaching working with refugee and other students with limited forma schooling.

http://teachingrefugees.com

The Teacher's Corner This site provides free generators to make a more extensive range of worksheets including crossword puzzle generator, word search makers and cloze sentence activities. It is very quick and easy to use.

http://worksheets.theteacherscorner.net/make-your-own/fill-in-the-blank/

The visual dictionary Hundreds of clear illustrations for multiple topics. Teachers can click on any image to read and see more detailed information.

http://www.infovisual.info/

Victorian Department of Education and Early Childhood Development: Support for Refugee Students Teachers' resources and cultural background information.

http://www.education.vic.gov.au/school/teachers/teachingresources/diversity/eal/pages/ealsupportrefugee.aspx

Quizlet The site assists teachers to create flashcards and games for learning vocabulary and key concepts. It also provides a number of pre-existing examples.

http://quizlet.com/teachers

This list was prepared by Maya Cranitch, with input from other authors and from Jane Wallace, Refugee Student Programs Advisor, NSW Department of Education and Training

Note: All the websites listed in this section were accessed and found to be operational as of January 2015

STRADDLE:
Webfoot War Dog

JOHN EVANS

In memory of Straddle and of Joe,
two special spaniels

Published by:
PATERCHURCH PUBLICATIONS
8 Laws Street, Pembroke Dock, SA72 6DL
Tel: 01646 683041
www.paterchurch-publications.co.uk

Designed and printed by Forrest DWJ Print, Tel: 01646 685963

First printed: December 2012

ISBN: 978-1-870745-17-8

1 'PD' - Royal Air Force Station Pembroke Dock - at it wartime zenith.
Group Captain A. M. Carey Collection

INTRODUCTION

The stories surrounding Royal Air Force Station Pembroke Dock, its squadrons and units and, most importantly, the personnel who served here, have fascinated me for so many years.

Pembroke Dock has a long and remarkably varied military and maritime heritage, spanning two centuries of often turbulent times, and its 'flying boat chapter' is one which has been deeply embedded into local, national and international history.

Located in the far west of Wales, on the southern shore of the fiord-like Milford Haven Waterway, Pembroke Dock had unique connections with all three Armed Services. The RAF era - spanning just under 30 years - is the briefest of all the service involvements locally, but encompassed the crucial period of the Second World War.

During World War II RAF Pembroke Dock became the largest flying boat station in the world, with nearly 100 flying boats - mostly the famous four-engined Sunderland - here at one time in 1943.

Pembroke Dock - known in the maritime air world simply as 'PD' - was truly an international base in wartime, playing host to service personnel and units from many nations. It was home base for squadrons from many countries - they came and went as the tides and priorities of war fluctuated.

In November 1944 RAF Pembroke Dock welcomed No 422 Squadron, Royal Canadian Air Force, and with the unit came its Cocker Spaniel mascot, Straddle. He was to make his mark on 'PD' in the next few months!

My special interest in Straddle and his wartime story stems from very rewarding contacts I have established with former members of 422 Squadron as part of my researches into Pembroke Dock's aviation history.

In the early 1980s I linked up with 422's former medical officer, Dr David Stewart, residing in Winnipeg, Manitoba. At the end of the war, and with an uncertain future awaiting the squadron, David collected together a large number of photographs from the squadron's photographic section. These he compiled into albums which, 40 years on, he generously loaned to me, posting them from Canada. Over many late evenings I copied the photographs onto negatives and David's collection remains one of the most significant in my own archive.

I shall always be most grateful to David Stewart for allowing me access to this remarkable collection - and to trusting the postal services in both countries to handle the packages safely. David's collection includes many shots of social activities by 422 Squadron and feature Straddle in various roles - formal and very informal.

In addition I am greatly indebted to the 422 Squadron Association and particularly to its former Chairman, Jack Logan, for generously sending me copies of Straddle's Logbook - in all respects a unique and revealing document. Jack has also provided copies of so many of the photographs and has helped in so many ways. The logbook is a treasured possession in my collection, and indeed in the Pembroke Dock Sunderland Trust Archive, and has been drawn upon heavily in compiling 'Straddle, Webfoot War Dog'.

John Evans
Pembroke Dock
October 2012

2

3

2 **Flight Lieutenant Arnold Jones with little Dinghy.**

3 **Straddle's mum, Whiskey.**

4 **Dinghy sitting pretty.**

4

1 Family Tree

Leafing though the histories of so many military units one often finds references to mascots; usually dogs but on occasions more exotic animals. Photographs of formal squadron groups - from the earliest days of military aviation - so often include one, or more, dogs posing alongside their masters.

Among the squadrons to adopt a mascot in World War II was No 422 Squadron, Royal Canadian Air Force - one of two RCAF units to fly that most famous of all the flying boats, the Short Sunderland, the other being No 423.

The squadron began forming up at Lough Erne, Northern Ireland, in May and June 1942 and was originally destined to fly the twin-engined Catalina. As these were in short supply the new CO, Wing Commander Larry Skey, DFC, arranged to 'borrow' seven little used Lerwicks - a twin engined monoplane flying boat that looked like a cut down version of the Sunderland. The luckless Lerwick did not enjoy the same enviable and deserved reputation as its bigger, four-engined sister.

After dallying briefly with the Lerwick the squadron did begin to take on the American-built Catalina but this association, too, was shortlived. Plans changed in October 1942 and 422 began to re-equip with Sunderlands. By then the squadron had relocated to RAF Oban, on Scotland's wild western coast where 422 became operational from 1st March 1943.

It was at Oban early in the new year that 422 took on a most important new recruit, an English Cocker Spaniel. Soon given an appropriate maritime name, 'Dinghy', the new arrival was in the best of care, his master being the squadron medical officer, Flight Lieutenant Arnold Jones.

Dinghy soon became a star in his own right, being trained to do party pieces like barking the correct number of times when playing cards were shown to him. He and his master would on occasions entertain with a programme of tricks.

From May 1943 the squadron operated from Bowmore, on Islay, again on Scotland's western side, before moving once more in the November, returning to Lough Erne - better known as RAF Castle Archdale. It was to be a very romantic and rewarding move for Dinghy. Limited accommodation meant that many 422 Squadron personnel were billeted at St Angelo, an RAF base some seven miles away, near Enniskillen in County Fermanagh. It was here that fate took a hand and Dinghy met Whiskey, a doe-eyed female spaniel owned by Squadron Leader Kent, the administration officer at the station. Dinghy - still less than a year old - became a dad when Whiskey produced six pups. The date was 5th January 1944.

One of the male pups was given to 422 Squadron by Squadron Leader Kent and was named Straddle. In maritime aviation 'straddle' has special resonance and meaning and was a term which flying boat personnel were very familiar with. When attacking German U-boats the intention was to 'straddle' the target, dropping depth charges each side of the vessel so that when they exploded they would rupture the hull and send the U-boat to the bottom. This required regular practice and successful execution of this very difficult form of attack often meant the difference between life and death.

Another term of special significance within the flying boat world was 'webfooter' - used to describe those who were connected with flying boats as it was claimed they often needed webfeet to do their duty!

Straddle - there could be no better name for a 'webfooted dog'.

5 **Early days for Straddle.**

6 **The badge of No 422 Squadron RCAF - Motto: This Arm Shall Do It.**
Sid Butler Collection

2 Feeling His Feet

Within a few days of his birth little Straddle was, unknowingly, already becoming a bit of a celebrity. A surprise visitor to St Angelo was Prince Bernhardt of the Netherlands when the Oxford communications aircraft carrying him was forced to land there - perhaps due to weather conditions. The Prince stayed in the quarters of 422's CO, sharing them with Dinghy, Straddle and the other pups. What the Prince made of the new arrivals, or if he even saw them, is not recorded.

Before the end of his first month in this world Straddle was beginning to enjoy his new status. At a social evening in the officers' mess little Straddle was fussed over by American officers stationed at a nearby camp. There was more involvement with North American cousins in February when American officers held a social evening in the Mess. Straddle, it was noted, attended *'to check on behaviour'*.

Changes were afoot as Flight Lieutenant Jones was posted to join another RCAF squadron, No 401, at Catterick in Yorkshire. Dinghy would be going too and on 5th March there was a dining out for Jones and three other officers who were all leaving the squadron.

With his father gone, the door was wide open for Straddle to become 422's Squadron Mascot. Exciting times were ahead!

Enter now the man who was to play such an indispensable part in the little dog's life - one of 422's pilots, Flying Officer Lloyd Detwiller. A British Columbian, Lloyd was at the time a member of the crew captained by Flying Officer Tomlinson. Known to all as 'Det', he became Straddle's new master, beginning a happy and at times eventful relationship which was to last into peacetime and a return to Canada.

And it was Det who created the unique logbook which detailed so many of Straddle's adventures and escapades as well as his flights, along with the changes and events that 422 Squadron was gripped by during the last 18 months of the war.

All this was charted in a standard issue logbook as used by all aircrew other than pilots. There was to be no other logbook like it in Coastal Command.

6

7

8

9

10

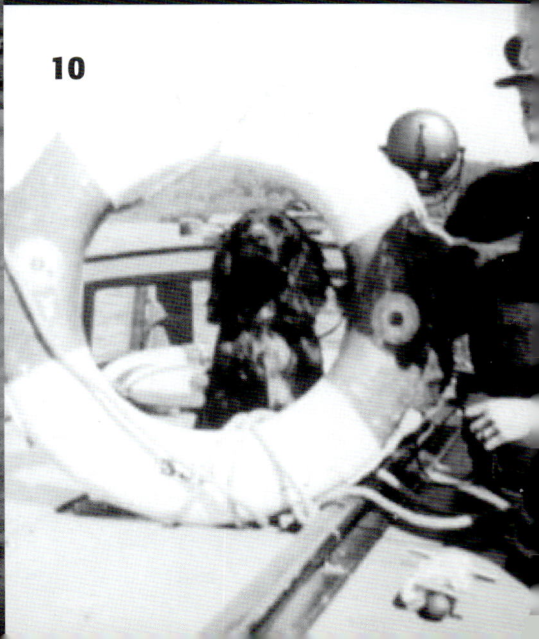

7 Sunderlands at Castle Archdale ready for D-Day.

8 Tea on the terrace, Skonk Hollow.

9 U-625 under attack.
Dr D. J. Stewart Collection

10 Straddle tries out a lifebelt.

3 Getting Airborne

By April 1944 No 422 Squadron was fully set up at Castle Archdale, its Sunderlands venturing out on long patrols to protect the Atlantic convoys and to search for U-boats. The squadron had had success against the U-boats the previous month when Flight Lieutenant Sid Butler, an RAF officer, sank U-625. At the time he was screen captain for Warrant Officer Morton and crew and remarkable photographs were taken of the copybook attack on the submarine. For this successful attack Butler was awarded the Distinguished Flying Cross (DFC).

Straddle's logbook records that on 13th April squadron personnel moved to Castle Archdale, adding: *'Everything turned upside down and Straddle goes along to supervise'*.

After being looked after for a time by Leading Aircraftsman Bob Baxter, and also staying with Flight Lieutenant Beattie in a hut in the officers' quarters, Straddle needed to find another home - and this turned out to be the oddly named 'Skonk Hollow' or Hut 203, typical wartime 'nissen hut' accommodation as found on so many flying stations.

Here he fell in with the six new occupants, including Det. The logbook records the original six members of Hut 203 - all Flying Officers - as Johnston, Detwiller, Tomlinson, Stukus, Stevens and Tustin. This would be 'home from home' for over six months.

Among Straddle's first duties was to visit injured airman George Fleming who was recuperating in an American military hospital after surviving a crash in February. Straddle went along, it was noted, *'with the gals that keep (him) supplied with steaks'*.

Sunderland W6028 had crashed in the Fermanagh countryside when on a fighter affiliation exercise, killing two of the crew and injuring several others. Among those injured was Det himself, the first pilot of this crew.

More socialising took place as the days lengthened and with warmer weather, the logbook recording that on 10th May Straddle *'serves tea to 14 on Skonk Hollow terrace'*. There was also another thing to look at and sniff around - Det had purchased an Austin 7 car and this was brought to the hut for overhaul, using parts scrounged from various sections in the camp.

May was also the month when Straddle began to get his 'webfooter' legs. On both the 16th and 21st of that month he was introduced to the Sunderland, and was on board for taxiing tests, showing good waterborne sense. After the second trip he went swimming in the Lough.

At the end of the month Det and a colleague headed off in the Austin - nicknamed 'Buttercup' - on leave, touring Northern Ireland. While they were away D-Day, the Invasion of Occupied Europe, began, on the 6th June. This was the start of an intense period of operations by 422 to support the Second Front.

With all the action taking place on the Normandy coastline there was minor drama at Castle Archdale - Straddle went walkabouts on the 8th June and was discovered locked in a hut on Davy Island, in the Lough. He was brought home and 'cleaned up' after his escapade.

It was high time for Straddle to become officially signed up and during June the People's Dispensary for Sick Animals (PDSA) was contacted in this connection. PDSA promptly responded and within days Straddle received his badge as a member of the Allied Forces Mascot Club, run by the PDSA. *

(* See Chapter 9).

Later in that momentous month of June Straddle officially joined the RCAF - at the exalted rank of Aircraftsman 6 (even lower than the lowest rank in the service, Aircraftsman 2!) He was also issued with his own service number, R000000, and a new collar which he promptly lost. It was found the next day and, as recorded in the logbook, replaced by a leather one. Straddle's formal arrival was announced in the Station Routine Orders and the title page of his logbook recorded that he had qualified as Mascot of 422 Squadron with effect from 16th of the month. To add authenticity, Squadron CO Wing Commander Joe Frizzle signed the page.

June was indeed quite a month for the pup and it ended with his first flight - and an operational one at that, on the lookout for enemy submarines. He joined Det's crew captained by Flight Lieutenant Harry Duggleby for what was a very long flight, totalling 14 hours 35 minutes, close to the maximum expected of a Sunderland.

The logbook stated: *'June 30th: Straddle's 1st ops trip, and first time airborne. Enjoyed whole trip very much and didn't relieve himself once in the 14:35 hours - but when he got on shore !!!! Good flying type'.*

Three days later Straddle was airborne again, and again with the Duggleby crew. This time they were aloft for 13 hours 35 minutes. *'Also very well behaved'* the logbook entry stated, *'weather a bit rough but didn't get air sick but glad to get onto ground again. Only trouble was when his ears blocked up suddenly while landing'.*

11 Bob Baxter, who looked after Straddle.

12 Sunderland 'J' 'ready to go'.

13 Hospital visit to George Fleming.

14 Skonk Hollow 'inmates'.

12

13

11

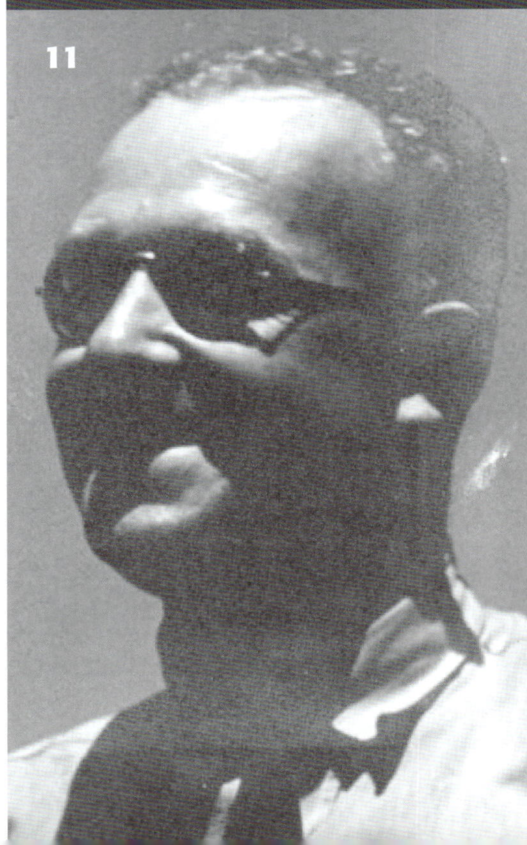

14

15

16

17

15 Checking the mid upper turret.

16 All set for another flight.

17 Straddle welcomes Smoky.

18 Sunderland ML884 in which Straddle flew.
Geoff Walker

18

4 Highs and Lows

July began with a squadron party in one of the hangars. Straddle went along but he was brought home early after doing too much barking. At least his head was clear in the morning, which could not be said for some of the other dance patrons. And it was back for a taxi test on board a Sunderland on 5th July, this time also to inspect and check out the turrets of Sunderland ML884, one of the ubiquitous Mark IIIs.

Straddle's third operational patrol in six days took place on 6th July in the now familiar ML884. It was flat calm at take off, always challenging for the crew in such conditions, and the weather was poor, restricting the anti submarine patrol to be flown at low level. When landing on return, Straddle's ears were not affected and he had a good time, sleeping well afterwards. Total flight time was just under 14 hours.

July was a milestone month in another way for the mascot. Straddle chose the BOAC hangar to 'cock his leg' for the first time. Now, said his logbook, *'he can be considered a real dog'*. When travelling in the car he got too excited after spotting rabbits and promptly jumped out, at 25 mph. No damage was done. On another occasion he collected paint on his head from a newly decorated door - Straddle was getting about.

Official duties for him in the month included a first session on the pinnace - from the RAF's marine craft section - for flare path duty with Det and others. According to the logbook Straddle had a say in deciding to scrub the night flying due to bad weather.

Further taxi tests were logged, in ML856 on 13th July, sharing the spacious Sunderland with 12 Air Training Corps cadets, for whom it must have been a bigger thrill than the now fairly seasoned dog mascot. And he joined Flying Officer Johnson and his team in ML836 on the 30th and apart from contemplating jumping down the galley hatch this was fairly uneventful.

There was also some unwelcome attention from the 'medics'. On 14th July, to treat a head cold, Straddle was given a dose of castor oil. He was his old self when he joined off duty Det and others for a picnic two days later, visiting Caldwell Castle, but the following day he had to sign off on sick leave and went to 'hospital' - with Enniskillen vet Mr Hardy. His return from 'detachment' at the vet's on the 21st was noted in the logbook - alongside a sobering entry recording the unsuccessful attempt made on Hitler's life in what is now known as the July Coup.

Straddle's bark was still affected by a tonsil problem but he was fighting fit to pose for photographs by a Sunderland mid upper turret, these for 'Wings' magazine. He also had a new friend, 'Smoky', another doggy pet - belonging to sister squadron 423 - who stayed overnight at Skonk Hollow. On 24th July the Air Officer Commanding No 15 Group of Coastal Command, Air Vice-Marshal Slatter, visited to present the squadron with its badge - an adorned arm holding a Tomahawk with the Motto 'This Arm Shall Do It'. It is not recorded if the AOC met with Straddle.

August opened with another taxi test with Det and Straddle mastered clambering up and down the deck stairs without falling. Although apparently on a 'starvation diet' he enjoyed his first taste of cottage cheese.

Discreetly, the logbook noted on 4th August that *'Straddle carries out small affair with MT girls'* - MT referring to Motor Transport section. Nothing further was added….. A few days later there were newcomers to the Skonk Hollow 'crew' - three chickens, named as 'Tom', 'Dick' and 'Harry'. Straddle was a bit jealous of the new arrivals! (They didn't last long, disappearing without trace on the 23rd though this was nothing to do with Straddle!)

Swims in the Lough on the 11th, and the excitement of finding 'Smoky' visiting, were too much for Straddle as he had what the logbook said was a 'slight fit' and had to be carried home to recover in his bed. A second attack three days later prompted a further visit to the Enniskillen vet who diagnosed teething fits, not distemper, and gave him pills. Back at base he was confined to barracks to rest and recuperate. By the 19th he was back to normal, to the relief of everyone.

During August five crews - including Det - and three aircraft from 422 and its sister squadron at Castle Archdale, 423, were detached to Sullom Voe in the Shetlands, returning on the 29th to a big welcome from Straddle and all. He also made friends with 'Big Jill', the larger than life doggy pet of the BOAC team.

There were new sights and smells for Straddle as September opened when he was taken to *'check over slipway and test odd telegraph pole. All found satisfactory'*. It appears that another operational flight followed on the 9th but the port outer engine went unserviceable and the crew returned to base early.

With Det his 'boss' away on leave, touring Ireland, Straddle was taken to the mess dance with music by the RCAF Dance Band. However, Straddle put up 'a bit of a black' but it is not recorded what he actually did. This was a time when many familiar faces on the squadron were posted, including some Skonk Hollow friends, and Squadron Leader Kent was another departure, returning to Canada.

On Det's return from leave Straddle did some taxi tests with his master who noted that the bark had become much stronger. Fleas were becoming quite an issue for Straddle and ended up with him being given a disinfectant bath which seemed to have sorted out the problem. Straddle's views on all this are unrecorded! As a hairy dog he also was given membership of the 'Bald Headed Club' - a little bald patch over an eye

2

19 Checking out the camp milk delivery.

20 Meeting 'Big Jill' of the BOAC team.

21 Presentation of badge to 422 Squadron.

22 Straddle get the 'gen' on the Pegasus engines.

earning him this dubious right in the Skonk Hollow Chapter of the club.

A few days later, in preparation for what was to come in the cockpit of a Sunderland, Straddle was given his first 'trip' in a Link Trainer - the stubby winged flight simulator which featured on every air station and where pilots kept up their instrument flying capabilities. It was a bit confusing but the logbook recorded that Straddle *'kept it from going into a spin'*.

The 'real thing' happened early in October when during the latest taxi test Straddle was checked out in the pilot's seat. This may have been the time when he was photographed sitting in the second pilot's position with Det in the captain's seat.

Early October also saw another night flare path duty with Det. This time the weather was kinder and they supervised the flare path and checked the anchorages - all important work. After a busy night Straddle slept all the next morning.

On 7th October Det did his first trip as captain but there was no place in the crew this time for the mascot. It was bombing practice and this was not good for a doggy stomach….. All in all a frustrating few days as earlier he had not been taken to an entertainment evening. There was time though for another taxi test and this time a run through on the Pegasus engines. If nothing else the training was thorough!

There were more comings and goings in October and an original occupant of Skonk Hollow, Flying Officer Stukus, departed for the other RCAF Sunderland unit, No 423. Only three of the six original occupants were now left but newcomers filled in the gaps and got to know their mascot.

Woodcutting details filled in some of the off duty time in late October. At the first Straddle it was noted *'was conspicuous by his absence'* with suggestions he was out with a lady friends (no names given). A few days later he had a wonderful time chasing in the woods on Tay Island while others gathering in a wood harvest. These were days of adventure for the spaniel.

23 Pembroke Dock aerial 1944 with Sunderlands on the water.
422 Squadron Association

24 Group Captain and Mrs Guy Bolland.

25 The location of the wing mounted APU.

26 New home at PD - a one-time married quarter.

27 Making the move by air.

5 Making A Mark At PD

Rumours of changes for the squadrons at Castle Archdale had been rife for a good time and in late October they became fact - 422 was to move from Ireland to Wales, to Pembroke Dock and the Milford Haven Waterway. There they would join an Australian squadron, No 461, and an RAF unit, No 228 - a cosmopolitan mix.

This coincided with a change of command on October 28th when Wing Commander J. R. Sumner took over from Wing Commander Frizzle. There was a big welcome party in the Mess and one dog had a surfeit of chicken for his supper. A couple of days later there was another party, to send off the old CO. A cross border sortie by car into the Irish Republic to buy liquor was accomplished and a good time was had by all.

The move of transferring an operational squadron from one base to another was a hugely complex one and on 3rd November Straddle was on hand to supervise the loading of aircraft with various equipment and stores. He just avoided falling into the water - a swim in an Irish lough in November was not to be chosen lightly.

The weather intervened again and the flights to PD were postponed, the strangely empty Skonk Hollow still being in use to the end. It proved a lucky break for Straddle. As the logbook gently put it: *'Straddle has first affair with 'Sally' (brown cocker). Will he prove himself a man?'*

On 7th November 25 people (and one dog) got airborne at last; destination west Wales. They had a good trip but encountered difficulties with the conditions in the tidal haven and were delayed in getting ashore and into their new billets. For Det and his charge it was Room 4 of what once had been the Married Men's quarters.

The logbook states: *'Very good spot but Straddle can't run quite as wild. Meets .... 'Paddy' and proceeds to take over the house. Is accused of wetting floor but it turns out to be small drip job from drinking out of fire bucket'.*

The Station Commander at PD was Group Captain Guy Bolland, a pre-war flying boat pilot. He readily gave permission for Straddle to stay on the camp, but within days no doubt was greatly regretting it...

'Raising hell' was the single line entry for 14th November before recording Straddle's escapades. *'Goes down to mess, into dining room, chases sheep down slipway, digs up tomato plants - all-in-all raises hell and ends up downtown with the dead end kids'.* The 'dead end kids' are not explained but very likely to be the local mutts with whom the mascot was fraternising. The results of all this mayhem? He was confined to his room for the rest of the day with orders to be tied up from now on - or else!

Two weeks later life had been restored to some form of normality allowing Det to take his charge up for another flight, this time a homing exercise. The logbook records: *'Bit nervous on take off but content if allowed to sit in pilot's seat. Fed before and after at flying ration stores'.*

A major happening in the RAF Station led to another logbook entry - for 30th November when the station clock tower, situated on the roof of one of the many fine Georgian dockyard buildings, went on fire and was burnt out (although the building was saved).

On 8th December - just five days before 422 resumed operational flights - a familiar face re-appeared in 422 circles; Flying Officer Stukus, one of the original Skonk Hollow hut crew, had returned to the fold, and to a doggy welcome.

28 Wedding congratulations for Roy and Doris Haines.
Group Captain Guy Bolland Collection

29 Dockyard clock tower well ablaze.
Group Captain Guy Bolland Collection

30 Armfuls! Warrant Officer Morton with Straddle and Sarg.

31 First birthday, January 5th 1945.

Straddle's first Christmas was eventful. He enjoyed his first Christmas dinner and there was also a dance on Christmas Day but the Station Commander was forced to close it because of the (large) crowd and all future dances were prohibited at Llanion (although it is not known if this was actually the case). The following day 422 held its own Squadron Party which was a great success. Training flights to Castle Archdale had proved profitable, with Irish turkeys on the menu - and the aftermath was lots of bones for one dog!

The seasonal festivities were too much for Straddle as he was not well as the new year dawned. He could not be tempted even by one of his steaks, but this proved irresistible to Det and a colleague who ate the steak as a midnight snack.

It was birthday celebrations for AC6 Straddle on 5th January, starting off with a run to the top of the hill (presumably the hill topped by the Victorian Defensible Barracks which was nearest the RAF base) and visits to various stores on the station. The celebrations should have continued into the evening with a party but one dog was too tired to take part. In his absence, and to 'convey Straddle's regrets', Det and his Navigator Bill Main visited some of the local pubs now becoming very familiar - the Royal Edinburgh, the Prince of Wales, Bush, Rose and Crown. Their noisy return to the billet disturbed the birthday boy.

Winter took a firm grip with gales on the 18th January and a couple of inches of snow falling on the 24th, prompting a big snow fight outside the Mess. The snow lay thick and all operations were closed down, with the whole station out enjoying the snow. As the logbook put it, a certain dog *'had a hell of a time...'*

In between the weather interventions there had been a trip on the Great Western railway to the seaside town of Tenby where Straddle had a fine time on the beach. However, at the Red Lion pub later he mixed it with a local, a terrier, and their scrap was only curtailed when beer was poured over them! There was no lasting damage from this fall out and Straddle did go on to attend a local dance to round off a good day.

The logbook records that the 'boss' - Detwiller - had finally got home by train from Plymouth after diverting there with a seized engine. In his absence Straddle and friends had enjoyed a visit to the Royal Edinburgh.

January ended with several of 422's aircraft in the wars through incidents like hitting a buoy, being damaged by marine craft and one running aground. Operating flying boats in often marginal weather was always challenging at PD, with its high tidal range and prevailing wind conditions.

If the logbook entry is anything to go by, Straddle - and others - certainly enjoyed the visit by Vicki Maier a WAAF (Women's Auxiliary Air Force) who came

30

31

to see them. *'Auntie Vicki visits Straddle in his palatial quarters. Hectic journey by bus, train, boat and foot and finally arrived safe to spend the night with him. Straddle fell for his new auntie (didn't we all!)'*, so says the logbook.

There were more celebrations in early February as 422's Flight Lieutenant Roy Haines married Canadian Doris Murphy, a Lieutenent Nursing Sister in the Queen Alexandra's Imperial Military Nursing Service at St John's, the parish church in Pembroke Dock. Following a very good party in the Officers' Mess the happy couple were loudly serenaded as a marine craft section pinnace took them away for their honeymoon. Straddle was kept in his quarters but managed to get in on the parade near the end. A 'casualty' of the party was the mess piano - it 'collapsed' the next morning!

On February 7th Lloyd Detwiller's promotion to Acting Flight Lieutenant was promulgated. A couple of days earlier he had taken a Sunderland to the Short Brothers factory at Windermere for modifications to Mark V standard, with the more powerful Pratt and Whitney radial engines.

Straddle was left behind and celebrated the promotion by chewing Bill Main's shaving brush in two - for which he *'got a small spank job'*. Main had also been promoted to the same rank.

It was back on the water soon after for both Straddle and another doggy pet. Straddle and 'Sarg', best of friends, went along to make sure all was ok for night take offs. Both apparently showed keen interest in starting the APU - the Auxiliary Power Unit, the Sunderland's fifth engine housed in the leading edge of the starboard wing.

On February 15th another flight was recorded in Straddle's logbook, the first trial of the secret sonobuoys, which was very successful. It was not a success for Straddle and it was perceived he had *'lost keenness for flying. Bit worried about whole affair and very glad to get down'*.

It was not all music to one's ears as a jam session in quarters on 17th February by Det, Flying Officer Platsko and Flight Lieutenant Nesbitt was howled down by a certain dog who barked all the time. The musicians were practicing for the squadron orchestra. Two days later a dance in the Officers' Mess was a great success. Straddle was locked in the billet for obvious reasons but had an early morning feast of left over cakes and sandwiches. And later in the month, in great weather, Straddle was on hand to help as a run was constructed for him in the back yard of 'home' - No9 Married Quarters. That evening he attended his first ENSA concert (in the RAF Chapel/Garrison Theatre) and enjoyed coffee and plum pudding in the room of squadron CO Wing Commander Sumner before going back to the theatre to check on the string quartet's rehearsals. This was a late session - he 'hit the sack' at 2.30 am!

32

33

32 Sunderlands ashore, Pembroke Dock.
33 Time out for Straddle and friends.
34 Fun time on the Barrack Hill.

34

6 Countdown To Peace

With the end of the European war in sight, work began to remove air raid shelters inside the RAF station and to restore a football pitch. There were blisters for the men involved in the hard work but no such problems for a couple of dogs. They had great fun.
The sharp end of PD's role was demonstrated on 28th February when Detwiller and crew were homed onto a sinking ship and to search for the U-boat which had attacked it. New sonobuoys were dropped but no submarine was located. The Sunderland crew saw the survivors from the ship being rescued before the aircraft was recalled to base.
'Luckily Straddle not along to cause confusion but told all about it on our return to Room 4 where he was waiting', says the logbook entry.
There was fun for Det and his crew, and dog, and lots of energy expended, in a football match (presumably on the newly cleared pitch). This was played on 1st March. *'Bags of exercise, just about killed ourselves, plus the dog in a football match. Photographic evidence of this affair to be exhibited to those questioning our whereabouts that day'* says the logbook.
Det and Crew 14 spent a couple of off duty days - and nights - at Tenby, returning to find Straddle sitting at the doorway waiting for them. And on 5th March Straddle joined Flight Lieutenant Dave Mills to fly a Sunderland back from the moorings at Angle Bay - it was common practice to make the short 'hop' from Angle Bay up to the RAF Station, rather than having the aircraft towed all the way. On arrival they met with Crew 14 who were on standby duty and ended up at the ration stores for bacon and eggs.
Big occasion for the Canadians was the opening of 'Canada House' - better known locally as Trinity Hall, at the rear of Trinity Church in Meyrick Street. Several airmen worked voluntarily for a month to decorate the rooms and senior officers and representatives of the community were invited along.
Also in parlance among the Canadians was B.O.B.C. - short for 'Brothers of the Bowden Cable' club - which formed around the turn of the year and took over the running of Llanion Barracks Canteen as a clubroom for its members. Here a most successful dance was staged on 6th March, the day before Det and crew went on leave to Torquay. They left their four legged crewmate in good hands, or so they thought……
Another black day for a black spaniel was 10th March, the logbook gravely noting: *'AC6 Straddle bugging the sheep. Goes off the deep end for the second time and chases the Group Captain's sheep which is not good. SPs (Service Police) pick him up and put him in the cooler. Rescued from a fate worse than death ……… (via the closed window) and is kept tied up outside No9'.* Chasing the Station Commander's sheep would certainly not endear him to the big boss!
Wisely, when the Air Officer Commanding made an inspection of the station a couple of days later, Straddle is kept well away from the top brass, but his loud barking could not be missed.
While all this was taking place 422 was carrying out intensive operations against the U-boats which were now operating using the schnorkel breathing apparatus, often close inshore. The good weather helped.
On his return from leave on March 26th Det heard all about Straddle's misdemeanours and he gave him a talking to, followed by a general clean up. And the search was on for a kennel.
At the end of March the Station CO, Group Captain Bolland, was posted and 422 held a cocktail party in his honour. With the

sheep incidents, and others firmly in mind, Straddle was not allowed to attend but sent his best wishes and a photograph of himself to remind the CO of his days at Pembroke Dock. There was consolation though that evening as Straddle went along to basketball practice, the team preparing for important finals in England. These took place days later with 422 losing their two games but the team had a lot of fun.

Daylight operations were restarted by the squadron but the first one was scrubbed due to the weather. Straddle and Det had a successful taxi test on 5th April, their aircraft being the first Mark V version on the squadron, fitted with Pratt and Whitney radials in place of the old Pegasus. Straddle was much in focus that afternoon, posing for many photographs all over the Sunderland. The Mark Vs were an instant success among the PD Webfooters, proving to be *'all that was expected'*.

A first visit to Canada House was enjoyed on the 6th, then up to Llanion Barracks on the other side of PD to join a big jam session in the mess at which Wing Commander Sumner led the choruses. Another squadron dance was held four days later but aircrew personnel attending were few due to the heavy flying programme. And the 422 Quartet (including Det) performed in the mess, receiving a hearty doggy welcome on return to quarters.

Sport was much on the agenda with the softball series due, and play-offs were held, leading up to a Saturday exhibition match. The first in the softball series opened with a concert by the RCAF Band from Bournemouth, followed by another concert in the Mess. Straddle enjoyed it all though the perfect weather meant it was a bit warm for him.

This was all recorded in the logbook, together with a one line

35 Straddle's photo presented to Group Captain Bolland.

36 The 422 Quartet hard at work.
Dr D. J. Stewart Collection

37 Removing air raid shelters - PD hangar behind.

38 Crew 14: Back, left to right: J. Bruce, B. Main, B. Patterson, L. Detwiller, B. Bowen, R. Pidcock. Front, L-R: V. Best, A. Berry, T. Chappell, S. Baker, J. Eadie.
422 Squadron Association

39 Straddle tries out the new B.O.B.C. truck.

57

8

9

entry - about the death of the US President, Franklin D. Roosevelt. Intriguingly the logbook also referred to a 'picture' entitled 'Coastal Command' in which Det's Crew 14 was cast. Scenes were shot using Sunderland 2-E in the 43 Group repair section. *'Bags of lights etc and Straddle stars with numerous scenes to himself'*. Some days later a film crew flew with Det and his team, filming a convoy patrol. (What became of this film is not known).

On 23rd April yet another dance was held in the Mess, enjoyed by all with Det afterwards bringing cakes home for his dog. The following day was Anzac Day and sister squadron at PD - the mainly Australian manned No 461 - began their Anzac Day celebrations with a banquet. An unscripted addition was a *'small shoot-up of Mess by the Mark Vs'*.

As German resistance finally crumbled in Europe the logbook included more references to the war situation. On 26th April news came through of the allied link up. *'Germany now split in two and the end must be near'*. The end indeed was near, with Germany surrendering on 3rd May, also recorded in the logbook.

Around this time 422 Squadron purchased a truck to be used for runs in connection with dances - as it turned out they would not have much time to use it.

New RAF Pembroke Dock CO, Group Captain W. H. Hutton, spoke to the station personnel and outlined policy for V (for Victory) Day and in the weeks to follow. Det had just been appointed squadron Adjutant (nicknamed 'Joe') and Straddle, confined to Det's office, put his signature - footprints - on all letters going to Group headquarters etc. The new Adj was not pleased!

Officially it appears, Detwiller was posted to 422 Squadron as Adjutant on 16th May, taking over from Flight Lieutenant Wilfey. Straddle became Assistant Adj .... *'and bugs everybody by his presence'*.

40

41

40 Straddle, complete with coat, leads the parade 24th May 1945.
Group Captain Guy Bolland Collection

41 Look right, not left - at Albion Square
Dr D. J. Stewart Collection

42 Station CO batting, Squadron CO catching
Dr D. J. Stewart Collection

42

7 Victory - And Uncertainty

'Looks like it's about all over' was the logbook entry for 6th May which noted that all German U-boats had been ordered to return to bases. *'Bags of gen on the surrender of the U-boats. V Day to be announced in a day or two'.* A church parade was held that same day.

The following day the victory celebrations began with Det and his quartet playing at dances. And there was a softball game (between the 'Ack-Acks' and the 'Bang-Bangs'), with Straddle leading the cheering. Bunting and flags appeared everywhere to bedeck Pembroke Dock's war-battered streets. The town had been heavily bombed in 1941 and showed many scars of the Luftwaffe's attentions.

There was a big 'do' in the Mess and signal flares fired from a hand gun - a Very Pistol - were let off by the dozen. Yet, as the logbook entry reflected….'

'Everybody felt it a bit of a letdown, like a job finished and now what?'

In RAF Pembroke Dock VE-Day on 8th May was marked by several social events in which Straddle played his part, ending up with a big feed in the Mess. *'Rather a good day all round'.*

The next day the celebrations continued with the townpeople letting their hair down. *'Street dancing, music, all types of merrymaking were evident. On the squadron another dance was held and also considerable pyrotechnics were used to give an impressive display of colour'.* The skies over Pembroke Dock - for so long subject to wartime blackout - were a riot of colourful streamers.

In the victory hour, with relief and joy all round, there came tragedy - as recorded in the logbook. Flying Officer B. C. Hunt, one of 422's flight engineers, died in hospital the day after he was run over on the slipway by an unmanned fuel truck which had rolled backwards. 'Benny' Hunt was 31 and hailed from Macleod, Alberta.

It had been three long, hard years since 422 had formed up at Castle Archdale and celebrations were in the air! Air Marshal G. O. Johnson, CB, MC, the Air Officer Commanding in Chief, Royal Canadian Air Force Overseas, was guest of honour at a dining in night on 23rd May to mark the third anniversary. The after dinner speeches gave strong indications of possible future roles for 422. Straddle, with past history of crossing paths with senior officers, was no doubt kept well out of the way of proceedings. That though was certainly not the case the day after when the Squadron celebrated in style, with the mascot playing a leading role.

'A perfect day' - that's how the logbook entry for the 24th May began. Air Marshal Johnson and party conducted a short tour of the station and then took the march past of the squadron in the town's Albion Square later that morning. *'Straddle at his best and wore his little coat and was the hit of the day'* - referring to the mascot's special role and the canvas coat, complete with squadron badge, which he wore. The 422 party was led by Straddle and his handler, marching at the head of the column from Llanion Barracks to the RAF Station. The new bugle and pipe band provided the stirring music.

The *West Wales Guardian* gave many column inches to the 'Canadians Parade', and Straddle got a very honourable mention. 'Much merriment was created by the sight of the squadron mascot, Pilot Officer Straddle, who in his own way scampered proudly along at the head of the parade'. The proud spaniel was now, by the way, a Commissioned Officer - Pilot Officer Straddle!

43

44

45

In the afternoon 422 Squadron beat its compatriots and arch rivals, 423, in a softball game with the 'top brass' opening the game. Air Marshal Johnson made the first pitch with Wing Commander Sumner catching and a mere Englishman, Group Captain Hutton, attempting the batting. It wasn't really cricket! In the evening there was a gala dance at Llanion Barracks where the decorations took the form of totem poles. The RCAF Streamliners provided the music and there were claims that this was *'the best dance ever held in PD'.*

'A great day for 422 and one we shall never forget', so said a special entry in the logbook.

Flying continued - and so did the rumours. The station church was the venue for a meeting when the news was broken that there were new horizons for 422 - but in Transport Command, not Coastal. And details were given of classes being set up by the squadron education officer.

In some of the last flights made by 422 Squadron Sunderlands the crews did low passes over the single funnelled troopship *Louis Pasteur* which was heading westwards carrying Canadians home. How soon the aircrews pondered would it be before they headed homeward too. There was, though, still the matter of a war out east to be finally won.

The last operational flight by 422 was made in one of the aircraft Straddle had flown in, Mark III ML884, Z for Zebra, on 30th May. Flight Lieutenant Stevens and his crew completed a 11 hour convoy escort flight.

Straddle's master had been away and on his return Det formally took over as Adjutant. With this new role came a move to accommodation in the main RAF Mess. Straddle, of course, went as well, and new roommate for them was 422's Medical Officer, 'Doc' Stewart.

The curtain fell on 422's long and meritorious wartime flying boat

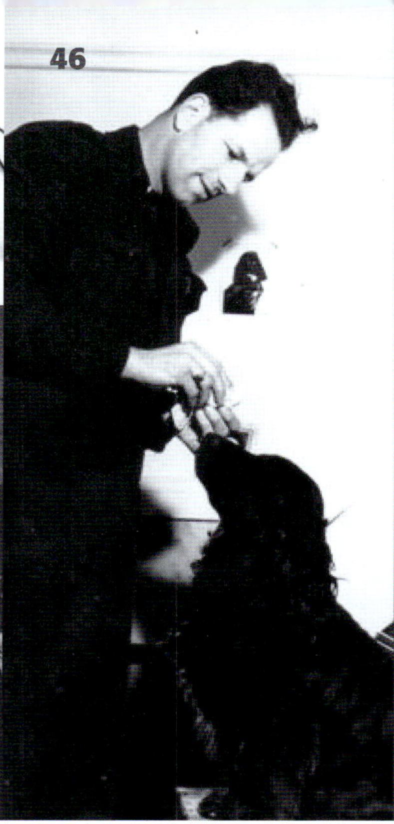

46

43 **Street victory celebrations.**

44 **Second Pilot Straddle, 5th June 1945.**

45 **RCAF Streamliners in full flight.**
Dr D. J. Stewart Collection

46 **Sprucing up for final visit to the 'Royal Edinburgh'.**

47 **Housemates Lloyd Detwiller and David Stewart.**
Dr D. J. Stewart Collection

48 **Heading home - the Louis Pasteur**
Dr D. J. Stewart Collection

47

48

chapter on 4th June when the order was received to ground all the aircraft. The break up of the squadron quickly began with RAF personnel posted out - aircrew and groundcrew who had played equal part in the many wartime episodes of a fine squadron in Coastal Command.

Straddle arrival at PD had 'raised a bit of hell', and he began to bow out in fine style, chasing cats up and down the mess but *'all in all fairly well behaved'*. Straddle also checked into the Royal Edinburgh Hotel *'to have a drink for the last time'.*

The logbook captured the mood: *'Many a tear dropped as the crews parted for the last time. Strange as it may seem, the feelings go pretty deep for the odd bods and sods in the individual crews'.*

Straddle also went to Defensible Barracks on top of the to bid farewell to old friends from Det's original Crew 12.

On 5th June Wing Commander Sumner and 422 Squadron were posted from Coastal to Transport Command. Heavy rain greeted those that struggled into breakfast and Straddle signed out of PD on a high - in more ways than one! *'Straddle tops it off by rolling in old fish adding to the confusion as he strolled through the mess dining hall'* - in what was almost the final entry in the logbook.

This was the milestone when the unique logbook record of a little black cocker spaniel, who had made such an impact and had experienced so many things in his 18 months of wartime life, was concluded. It also recorded, as for any airman, the total flying time. In Straddle's case he had flown 49 hours and 40 minutes by day, and seven hours and five minutes by night - a grand total of 56 hours 45 minutes. Straddle had certainly earned his 'wings'.

49

50

49 Straddle leads march to railway station.
Dr D. J. Stewart Collection

50 The Commanding Officer and Flight Commanders of 422 Squadron.
J. L. Watson

8 Promotion And Homecoming

The war in Europe was over but there were still hard fought campaigns to be won in Far Eastern skies. And this is to where the eyes of those remaining on 422 Squadron were turning.

'PD is but a ghost of its former self. Empty halls and anterooms where one's footsteps echo back….as we pass through rooms looking for remaining bodies. A few Sunderlands tug gently at their moorings impatient to be on their way again. The remaining squadron, 422, wanders about the camp….trying to keep busy'. This was penned anonymously - not in Straddle's logbook - and reflected the last days of 422 at Pembroke Dock.

On 24th July 1945 the Canadians finally said farewell to PD, entraining at the railway station and heading for RAF Bassingbourn, an air station in Cambridgeshire until recently occupied by the United States Army Air Force. This was now a Transport Command station and the aircraft there were Liberators - American-built four engined bombers destined to become part of the huge transport fleet to support the campaign by the RAF and its allies in the war against the Japanese. It was a move from keels to wheels for the men of 422.

Within a few days of the squadron's arrival the war situation changed dramatically with the dropping of the first atomic bomb by the Americans on Hiroshima, followed soon after by a second targeted on Nagasaki. The Japanese sued for peace and there was now no need for many of the Liberator units. Flying training on the Liberators continued until 27th August and then on 3rd September 1945 No 422 - along with its sister unit, No 423 - disbanded at Bassingbourn. Their work was done; it was time to go home, and with them went Straddle.

Now he was Pilot Officer Straddle, having been promoted to commissioned rank in April. And as an officer he had to be saluted by other ranks!

Daily Routine Orders for 12th May recorded an 'After Order' with stated: 'Mentioned in Dogspatches'! For completing one operational tour on sheep patrol and undergoing dangers of extermination - showing great initiative and complete disregard of all concerned'.

'Awards - To AC6 Straddle (now P/O) effective 1st May 1945, Authority, one ops wing'.

'Promotion - No 000000, AC6 Straddle, Squadron Mascot, appointed to commissioned rank on 27/04/45, Authority WXYZ/9876, dated 21st April 1945'.

It had long been planned that when Lloyd Detwiller returned to Canada Straddle would go to, and so it proved to be. They travelled on the troopship *Scythia* and Straddle made headlines in a newspaper story entitled 'Flier Brings Home Bemedalled Cocker', together with a photo of the dog wearing a life jacket.

The report went on: 'A new citizen will come to Vancouver on Saturday with a group of citizens who have been away at the wars for the past few years.

'He is First Pilot Officer Straddle, official mascot of 422 Squadron RCAF who has 94 hours of operations on Sunderland flying boats, convoys and anti submarine patrols to his credit' (the 94 hours quoted is at variance to the logbook total).

The report added that Straddle was entitled to wear the 'ops' medal for 18 months service with the squadron, and had the Canadian Volunteer Medal, 1939-45 Star, Defence Medal and Atlantic Star'.

Straddle's new home was with Lloyd Detwiller and family at 6550 East Boulevard, Vancouver, on Canada's western coast. Here he was issued with a dog licence by the City of Vancouver,

51

53

54

55

52

51, 52, 53
Before leaving Pembroke Dock 422 Squadron had a beach party at Broad Haven, near Bosherston, and Straddle had great fun, even allowing himself to be buried up to his neck in sand. He survived!
Dr D. J. Stewart Collection

54 One of the Liberators flown briefly by the Squadron
Dr D. J. Stewart Collection

55 Cunard liner *Scythia* used as a wartime troopship.
Author's Collection

56 Newspaper welcome for Straddle.

56

MEET "PILOT OFFICER STRADDLE," official mascot of No. 422 Squadron, RCAF. He sits aboard the troopship, Scythia, wondering when he will arrive in his new Canadian home. He'll be taking out citizenship papers to reside with his owner, Flt.-Lt. L. F. Detwiller, 6550 East Boulevard, Vancouver.

Flier Brings Home Bemedalled Cocker

A new citizen will come to Vancouver Saturday with a group of citizens who have been away at the wars for the past few years.

He is First Pilot Officer "Straddle," official mascot of No. 422 Squadron RCAF, who has 94 hours of operations on Sunderland flying boats, convoys and anti-submarine patrols to his credit.

WEARS RIBBONS

He has the distinction of having been "Mentioned in Dog Dispatches" and is entitled to wear the "ops" medal for 18 months' service with the squadron.

"Straddle is a cocker spaniel, born in Northern Ireland two years ago and "bred in the blue." His owner is Flt.-Lt. L. F. Detwiller, 6550 East Boulevard, RCAF pilot.

"Straddle" was enlisted as aircrafman, sixth class, with number R000000.

After completing a tour of "ops" with his owner he was promoted to pilot officer and given number J000000. At the same time he was "Mentioned in Dog Dispatches."

'A GREAT GUY'

On Straddle's head are the Canadian Volunteer Medal, 1939-45 Star, Defense Medal and Atlantic Star.

"He's a great guy," says Detwiller. "During our swoops in the Sunderlands he used to wander all over the aircraft visiting the boys. Sometimes these trips

costing two dollars and 20 cents.

In contrast to his earlier life in wartime locations Straddle settled down in his new surroundings but there was to be no happy ending to this story. In August 1948, less than three years after arriving in Canada, he died after being hit by a car in Vancouver. As a 422 Squadron Newsletter recorded many years later: 'Unfortunately, the light traffic of Pembroke Dock did not train the mascot for the greater activity of the streets of a large city…' A tragic ending for a dog who had become something of a legend in his short life. RIP Straddle.

57

58

57, 58

Regal pose by Straddle, wearing his PDSA Allied Forces Mascot Club badge.

9 Mascot Club

During World War II the Allied Forces Mascot Club registered many members to the club, and Straddle was enrolled on 16th June 1944. The Mascot Club was run from the PDSA's north west area office in north London. From there the Club Secretary, Dorothea St Hill Bourne, wrote to Lloyd Detwiller, enclosing the badge of membership.

She went on: "I am so glad we were able to get in touch with you and, when there is an opportunity, we shall be pleased to have further details of Straddle - his adventures, characteristics and so on - in fact any stories of his career it is possible to have without infringing security regulations. Also, circumstances permitting, we should like to have a picture of him; we have many snapshots and photographs of members and these are included in our records."

The letter concluded: "Wishing Straddle and all his Unit the very best of luck."

Straddle became Allied Forces Mascot Club member No 603, complete with splendid dog tag!

The formal enrolment of Mascot Club member No 603 was mentioned in squadron orders soon after and Straddle was officially able to draw rations with effect from 16th June 1944!

In early 1945 Straddle's master wrote to the Mascot Club and enclosed two photographs. This prompted a further letter from Dorothea St Hill Bourne in which she hoped Det would be able to take Straddle back to Canada and provided helpful advice on whom to contact at the Ministry of Agriculture and Fisheries.

"How is Straddle getting on these days; is he following in his famous father's paw-steps?" she asked. "We are always very interested to have news of our members. We are very pleased to have the two charming snapshots of him. With best wishes to Straddle and to his Unit."

Final correspondence between Straddle's owner and the Mascot Club came in mid August 1945 following notification of change of address to RAF Bassingbourn. A new badge was also sent to replace the old one (it is not known if Straddle's first badge had been lost).

"I expect Straddle is thrilled at the idea of getting back to Civvy Street," wrote Dorothea St Hill Bourne, who also enquired about Straddle's father, Dinghy, as she had not heard of him for a long time.

Dinghy, too, had an eventful war and went to France with his master, 'Doc' Jones. When 401 Squadron - a fighter unit with Spitfires - went to France after D-Day, Dingy and 'Doc' Jones went too. It is recorded that Dinghy went in style - in the cockpit of a Spitfire! From superb Sunderlands to supreme Spitfires, Dinghy had flown in the best!

An undated newspaper cutting shows Dinghy riding on a motorcycle with his owner. He, too, went to Canada after the war's end. She wrote:

Both Cocker Spaniels, father and son, are mentioned in Dorothea St Hill Bourne's book entitled *'They Also Serve'* published soon after the war.

'When Dinghy, a sleek black cocker pup, was born in the Isle of Mull, he was blessed with a remarkable number of gifts and accomplishments, and an unusual beauty.

'At six weeks old he was adopted by Flight Lieutenant A. F. 'Doc' Jones. A week later he became a mascot of a RCAF squadron in Islay and began a wonderful friendship with his master in addition to embarking on a career which made him famous.

'He broadcast for the BBC and was 'shot' in a newsreel. He

STRADDLE, flying mascot of 422 Squadron, Royal Canadian Air Force.

DINGHY, father of Straddle, and also mascot of an R.C.A.F. Squadron.

entertained troops from north Scotland to southern England and in Northern Ireland too. And what did Dinghy do? It would be easier to say what Dinghy didn't do rather than what he did. Besides being by profession a perfectly trained gun dog, he was a first class amateur entertainer. He performed every possible trick which an intelligent dog delights in doing for his master. He could die for his country, could open and shut doors, would eat and drink only on the word of command, shake hands, and so forth.

'Dinghy was an accomplished mathematician and did sums, barking out the correct answers. He could bark the number of days in a week, weeks in a year and the number of 'kills' made by his squadron'.

Referring to Straddle the author went on: 'Straddle took over as mascot of 422 Squadron when his father was transferred to 401 Squadron. He carried out his duties successfully, although he did

59 Illustrations from 'They Also Serve'. *Author's Collection*

60 Newspaper picture of Dinghy and his owner, in France.

RCAF Pets Travel to France

60

Dinghy, born in the Hebrides, went to Scotland, back home, then to Ulster and to England, and now he's in France riding again on the motorbike of his owner, Flt. Lt. Arnold Jones, Montreal.

not prove so good at mathematics and Dinghy's other accomplishments. Straddle had his own logbook from the time of his birth. In it were recorded several operational trips. He served first with Coastal Command and when later his squadron took on transport duties, Straddle prepared for trips to India.

'On demobilisation both Dinghy and Straddle sailed for Canada with their masters'.

In post-war Montreal Dinghy continued his entertainment career, performing for a number of years alongside his owner for service organisations and others. In 1952 Dinghy was made a life member of the RCAF Association in appreciation of his services in both wartime and peacetime. That year he travelled frequently with an RCAF unit which was recruiting volunteers for the Ground Observer Corps.

61

62

61 Straddle Mark II - 'Joe' - with 'RCAF minder' Judith Davies.
Martin Cavaney Photography

62 'Joe' again, with Straddle model and its creator John Arcus
Martin Cavaney Photography

10 Straddle Mark II

The story of Straddle lives on both in Canada, through the 422 Squadron Association and the memories of those who served on the squadron at the time, and at Pembroke Dock's unique Flying Boat Centre, run by the town's Sunderland Trust.

Pembroke Dock was known simply as 'PD' among all involved with flying boats - and in wartime it became the largest operational flying boat station in the world.

Although the town's maritime aviation chapter ended in the late 1950s, when the famous Sunderlands were finally pensioned off from RAF service, the legacy of the golden era of flying boats has continued and has become a tourist attraction in its own right.

In the 1980s and 1990s five very successful Flying Boat Reunions were staged at PD, bringing many hundreds of 'webfooters' back to the town. These reunions, and several theme weeks staged during this period, led to the development of the Gun Tower Museum - in an historic Victorian waterfront fort - and in 2009 to the opening of the UK's only Flying Boat Centre. This is located in a workshop building in the former Royal Dockyard and has many displays relating to Royal Air Force Pembroke Dock and its 30 years of flying boat history. Straddle's story is one of those featured in the Centre.

Over the years strong links have been maintained between the 422 Squadron Association in Canada and Pembroke Dock and the Association has contributed important artefacts to the 'Pembroke Dock Collection'. Uniquely, some of these relate to Straddle and include the canvas coat that the mascot wore in 1945 when he led the parade through the town to mark the squadron's third anniversary.

The coat was donated to the Pembroke Dock Sunderland Trust by the 422 Association, having been gifted by the Detwiller family in Vancouver. It is in remarkable condition, still with the coloured crest of the squadron, and had been kept in excellent condition by the family.

Along with the coat came other items from the Detwiller family, including Straddle's leather lead and badge.

Now enter 'Joe', a black cocker spaniel belonging to Pembroke Dock Sunderland Trustee Martin Cavaney. Joe was 'called up' to stage as 'Straddle Mark II' for the official opening of the Flying Boat Centre in September 2009. For this he wore Straddle's coat and was a star of the show, helped by the Project Administrator Judith Davies who donned a genuine World War II Royal Canadian Air Force uniform, generously donated to the Trust by Mrs Jean Doern and family of Winnipeg, Manitoba, Canada, in memory of Doug Doern who served on 422 Squadron.

So Straddle lives on at the Flying Boat Centre, not only through photographs and words in a display panel which tells his story but also as a lifesize model which sits on the donations box at the Centre. In fibreglass, it was created by John Arcus who at the time was working for the Milford Haven Port Authority in support of the Sunderland Trust.

Straddle, the little dog who went to war, and his story will never be forgotten.

63 January 1945 and a moment frozen in time after a blizzard swept across Pembrokeshire. Very rarely in this mild maritime climate does snow transform the low lying lands around the Milford Haven waterway. The white-hulled Sunderlands blend into the snowclad landscape.
Group Captain Guy Bolland Collection

64 422 Squadron line up before one of Pembroke Dock's hangars.
422 Squadron Association

What A Swell Time...

Straddle's logbook includes a poignant poem penned by Warrant Officer L. B. Frederick .... 'who', the introduction stated, 'has put down on paper what we all feel. As we look out over the 'Haven' and see the good old Mark IIIs resting in the water, tugging slightly at their mooring as much as to say they want to keep going, one can't help but feel a lump rise up in the proverbial throat and think what a swell time we have had together'.

The Pilot's Farewell

The tumult and the shouting die,
And all is still.
While idle on the waters lie
My once proud kite,
As waterfowl bewitched await the kill.

That sleek and deadly bird of prey,
I loved so well,
Instead of white, looks deathly grey;
Her heart is gone,
And heartless, she is but any empty shell.

In peace her fiery horses rest,
Their great work done;
They gave me of their very best
In cold and storm,
And roared approval when a fight was won.

Deserted now, she seeks my face
And gentle hand;
With eager longing for the race
She strains her bonds,
To seek and win the prize of my command.

Alas, no longer will she know
My vibrant voice,
As winging o'er the waves we go;
No longer now
With me upon return will she rejoice.

The die is cast, the job is done,
And we must part;
But though our partnership has run
The sands of time,
Where'er you fly, dear wings, you take my heart.

L. B. Frederick
422 Squadron, June 1945

65 The title page of Straddle's logbook, certifying his Mascot qualifications between June 1944 and July 1945.

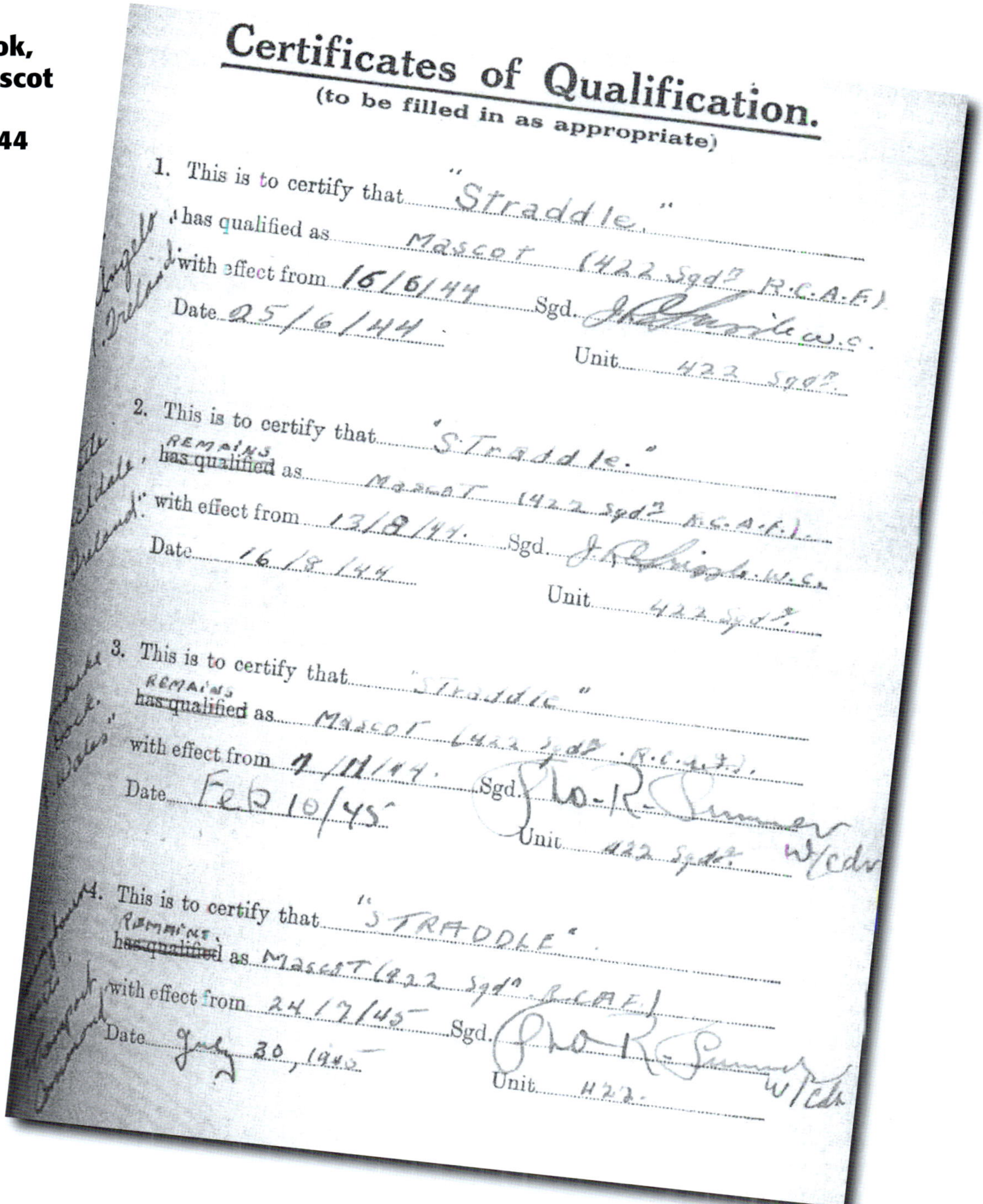

Certificates of Qualification.

(to be filled in as appropriate)

1. This is to certify that "Straddle." has qualified as Mascot (422 Sqdn R.C.A.F.) with effect from 16/6/44 Date 25/6/44 Sgd. [illegible] W.C. Unit 422 Sqdn

2. This is to certify that "Straddle." ~~has qualified~~ REMAINS as Mascot (422 Sqdn R.C.A.F.) with effect from 13/8/44. Date 16/8/44 Sgd. [illegible] W.C. Unit 422 Sqdn

3. This is to certify that "Straddle" ~~has qualified~~ REMAINS as Mascot (422 Sqdn R.C.A.F.) with effect from 7/11/44. Date Feb 10/45 Sgd. [illegible] W/Cdr Unit 422 Sqdn

4. This is to certify that "STRADDLE". ~~has qualified~~ REMAINS as Mascot (422 Sqdn R.C.A.F.) with effect from 24/7/45 Date July 30, 1945 Sgd. [illegible] W/Cdr Unit 422.

ACKNOWLEDGEMENTS

The generous donation of copies of Straddle's logbook by the 422 Squadron Association in Canada has made this book possible, together with the key support of Jack Logan, former Chairman of the Association. Jack has provided copies of so many of the photographs in the logbook and has made many helpful comments on the text. His help is especially acknowledged.

Special thanks also go to the Detwiller family in Vancouver, British Columbia, whose donation of Straddle's coat - which he wore on parade in 1945 - and other artefacts, further brought this story to life. These items, received through the Squadron Association, are now part of the Pembroke Dock Sunderland Trust Archive. Another important link between Pembroke Dock and 422 Squadron is the uniform worn by the late Doug Doern - kindly donated to the Sunderland Trust by Mrs Jean Doern and family, of Winnipeg, Manitoba.

'Straddle's Story' has been long talked about by myself but it has taken the encouragement of my wife, Christine, to see it actually happen. So this is for her as well, and for my ever supportive family.

In my usual very short timescale Amanda Griffiths and Andrew Forrest, of Forrest DWJ Print, have quickly designed and produced this book. My thanks to them for their skills and expertise.

The photographs used are all from Straddle's logbook, via Jack Logan, unless otherwise credited.

John Evans
Pembroke Dock, October 2012

ABOUT THE AUTHOR

A journalist by profession, John Evans has lived in Pembroke Dock for over 30 years and has specialised in researching flying boats - particularly the Sunderland - and the story of Royal Air Force Station Pembroke Dock. He has been involved in heritage initiatives in the community for many years, including the Gun Tower Museum and in establishing the Pembroke Dock Sunderland Trust and the UK's only Flying Boat Centre.

Also by the Author and Paterchurch Publications

Flying Boat Haven (Pictorial of RAF Pembroke Dock)

Three pictorials on the Sunderland:

The Sunderland, Flying Boat Queen Vol I

The Sunderland, Flying Boat Queen Vol 2

The Sunderland, Flying Boat Queen Vol 3

Help From The Heavens (History of 228 Squadron, RAF)

Sopwiths to Sunderlands (History of 210 Squadron, RAF)

Pembroke Dock Reflections (Pictorial of PD in the 20th century)

Final Flights, Vols I and 2 (Aircraft accidents and losses in west Wales)

PATERCHURCH PUBLICATIONS
8 Laws Street, Pembroke Dock, SA72 6DL
Tel: 01646 683041
www.paterchurch-publications.co.uk

Back Cover: In this delightful cartoon - which features in the logbook - Straddle and his kennel get airborne as the Skonk Hollow crew take to the lanes around Castle Archdale.

Iela Mari

Eat and Be Eaten

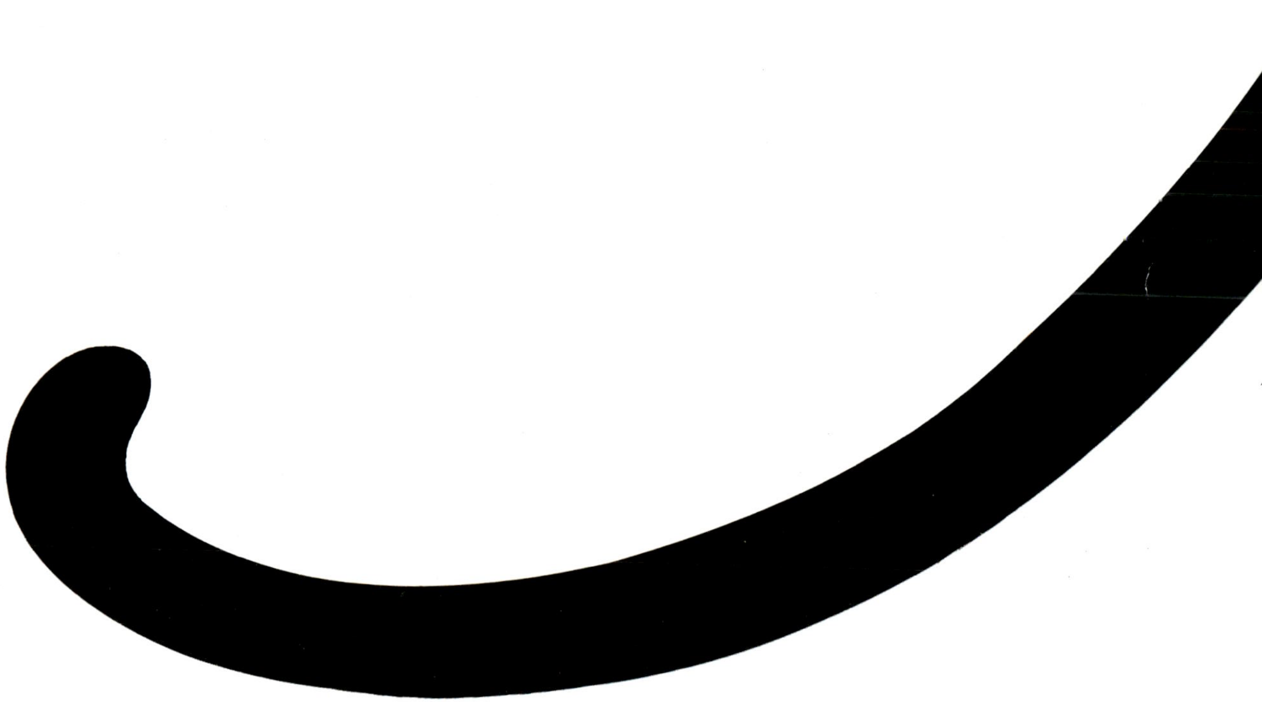

J M Dent & Sons Ltd London Toronto Melbourne

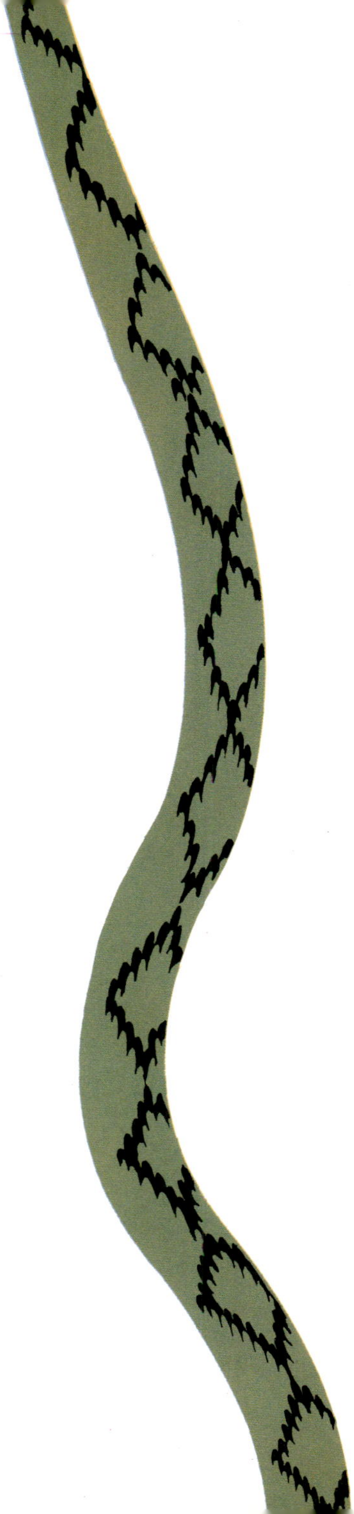

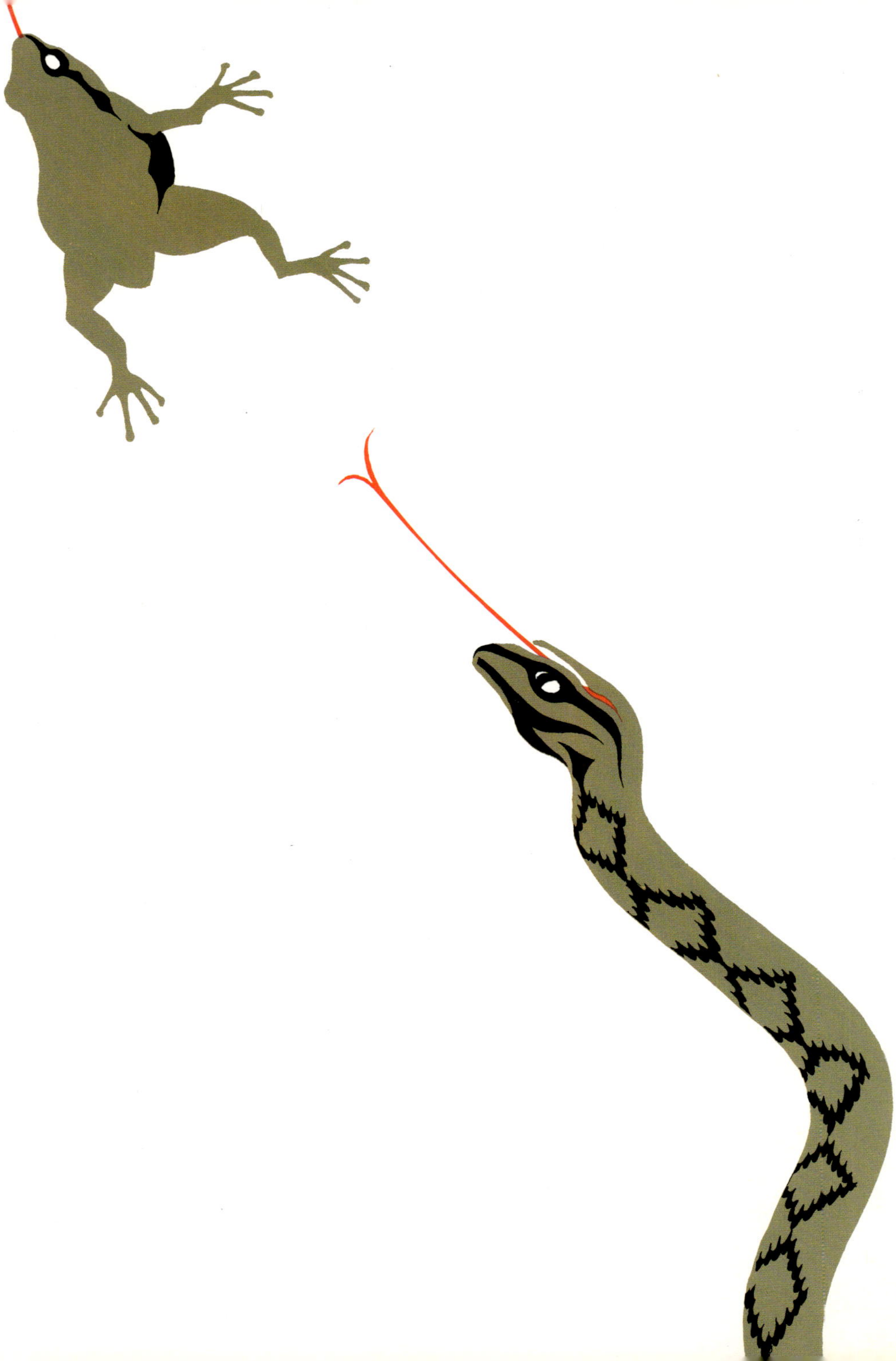

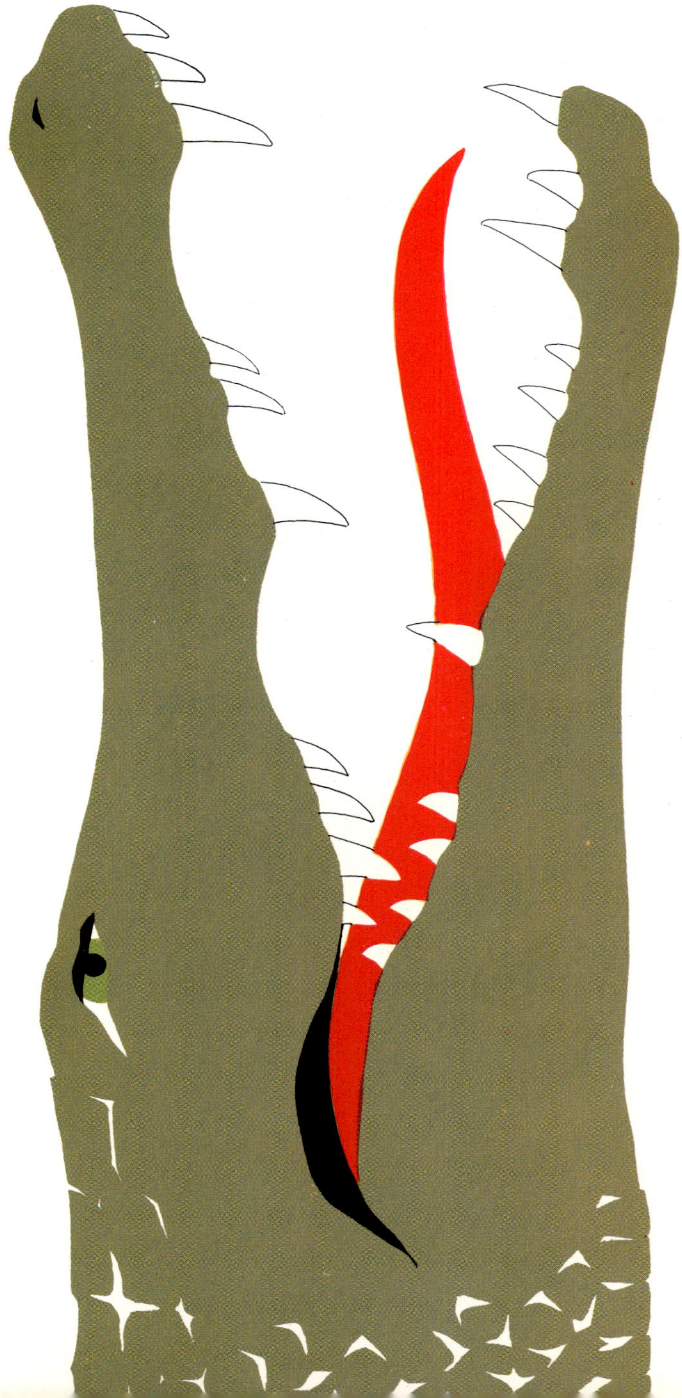

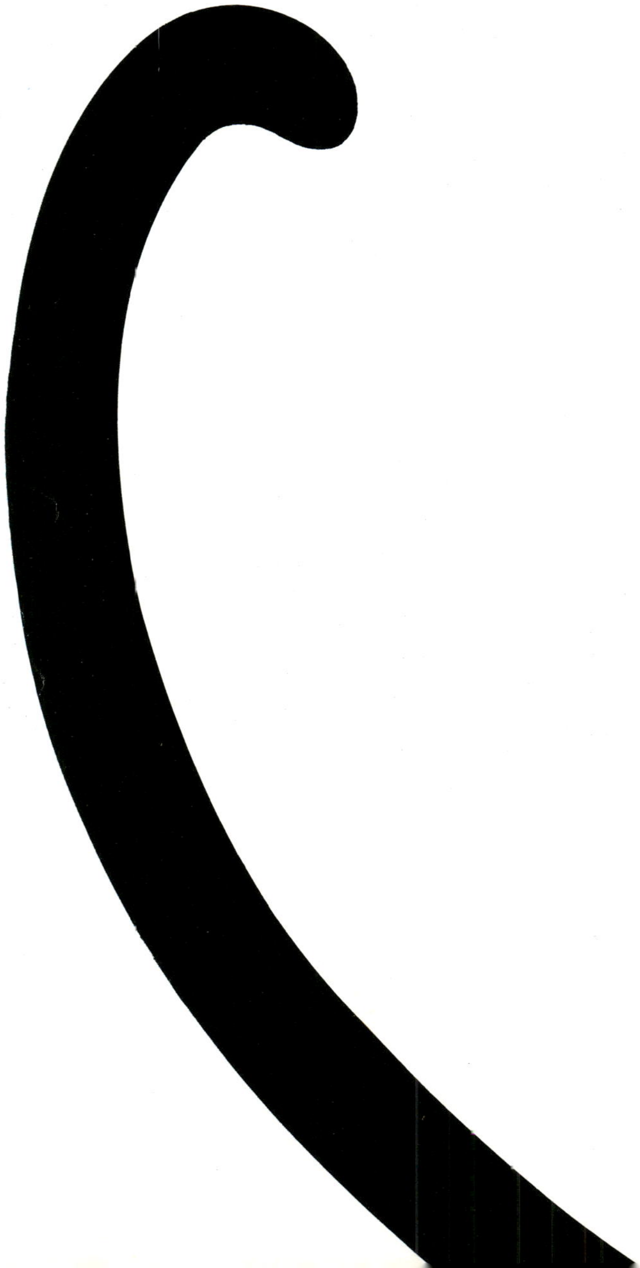